The PATH to Strategic Impact

What Great Leaders Understand about Strategy Communication (and Others Don't)

Dr. Michael Gerharz

Foreword by Alex M H Smith

The PATH to Strategic Impact: What Great Leaders Understand about Strategy Communication (and Others Don't)
Dr. Michael Gerharz
53842 Troisdorf, Kantstr. 12, Germany

Copyright © 2024 by Dr. Michael Gerharz. All rights reserved.

No part of this book may be reproduced in any form or by any mechanical means, including information storage and retrieval systems without permission in writing from the publisher/author, except by a reviewer who may quote passages in a review.

ISBN: 979-8-3290-1341-2 (paperback)
ISBN: 979-8-3290-1385-6 (hardcover)

BUSINESS & ECONOMICS/Strategic Planning

Cover and interior design by Rachel Valliere

B# PUBLICATIONS

B Sharp Publications

For Stephanie

Contents

Foreword ix

Introduction: The Strategy Gap 1

Part 1: Understanding Strategy Communication

1 The PATH to Strategic Impact 11
   Wait! What Actually Is Strategy? 13
   How Communication Can Ruin Strategy 15
   Case Study: The Power of Alignment 17
   The Impact of a Clear PATH 19

2 P is for Plain and Simple:
   Understanding How to Make Choices 23
   A Myriad of Choices in a Demanding Environment 25
   The Core Credo 26
   Case Study: Capturing the Spirit of the Strategy 27

The Perfect Representative. 28
It's Not About Being Fancy. It's About Being Clear. 30
How to Find Plain and Simple Words for Your Strategy. . 31
Conclusion 33

3 A is for Actionable:
Making the Right Choices Stand Out. 35
What Makes a Strategy Actionable? 36
Case Study: The Power of Obvious Choices 38
The Lazy Strategy: Concrete but not Actionable. 40
The Nuances of "Good Judgment". 41
How to Find Actionable Words to Communicate
   Your Strategy 42
Conclusion 44

4 T is for Transformative:
Encouraging Bold Choices 47
Case Study: Making the Impossible Possible 48
The Ripple Effect of Transformative Strategies. 50
Case Study: No Transformation Without the Team 51
How to Find Transformative Words for Your Strategy . . . 53
Conclusion 55

5 H is for Heartfelt:
Getting Passionate About Your Choices 57
Case Study: Trusting the Team 58
The Sustainable Fuel: Passion and Commitment 60
The Power of Identification 61

How to Find Heartfelt Words to Communicate
Your Strategy 63
Conclusion 65

Part 2: Applying the PATH Approach in Your Organization

6 Choosing Your PATH 69
Finding the Courage to Focus and Amplify 71
The Path to Getting it Right 74
Tapping into Your Team's Brilliance 76
Your PATH Awaits 78

7 Navigating Your PATH 79
Navigating Complex Organizational Dynamics 80
Navigating Scalability Challenges 85
Maintaining Flexibility 89
Changing Direction 91
Conclusion 93

8 Lighting the PATH 95
Filling the PATH with Meaning 96
Can They See it? 99
Ingraining Your PATH into Your Culture 100
Not Compliance, but Connection 103

9 True Progress 105

Appendix

Appendix A: The PATH to Strategic Impact in a Nutshell..109
1. Plain and Simple........................... 110
2. Actionable.................................111
3. Transformative...........................112
4. Heartfelt..................................113
Implementation and Review..................114

Appendix B: Glossary: From Vision to Strategy . . . 115

Appendix C: Further Reading..................117

Acknowledgments............................ 121
About the Author 123

Foreword

David Perell wrote, "The world doesn't reward the people with the best ideas, it rewards the people who are best at communicating ideas." And with every passing day as a peddler of ideas, I find this to be more and more true.

In some fields, this truth isn't necessarily a problem. The people selling ideas understand it, and behave accordingly. But there is one field where it is a problem, a huge one: strategy. I don't know what it is, but there's something about self-described "strategists" that makes them feel they are somehow "above" good communication. Above style. Above sizzle. Above sex appeal. Above all the stuff that, if we're honest, actually makes things happen. Perhaps they think that good communication is somehow manipulative—that it sells ideas that can't sell themselves? Or perhaps they think that the "right" strategy will just insist on itself, and so the notion of communicating it effectively just never comes up?

Either way, they are wrong. Even the best ideas are only as good as how they are communicated.

I think it's important we remember what strategy actually is. Strategy is nothing more than a *precursor* to action. It can be judged on one thing, and one thing alone: did it get people to *act*?

You can't judge it by intelligence and rigour. Some of the greatest strategies ever were sketched on the back of a napkin. And you can't judge it by results, as often they are at the mercy of various factors out of your hands.

No, action is the *only* output. And so if you want to get people to act, you need to call on *all* the tools which are known to do that. The very tools outlined in this book.

Heck, it sounds crazy, but I would argue that a well-communicated "bad strategy" is a hell of a lot better than a poorly communicated "good one." After all, at least with the former *something* will happen—whilst the latter will only gather dust in a desk drawer. And once you start making things happen? Well, you have no idea what the effects might be. It might be that your "bad strategy" succeeds in ways that you never anticipated or planned for.

This is why, in my own strategy practice, I have shifted the emphasis of my projects away from substance and towards style. Being clever is important. But being charismatic is essential.

So it's super refreshing to see a book that finally addresses this hidden urgency in the strategic game. Until today, most people have only been doing half a job. This book represents the missing half. Master it, and your strategies may not be any "better"… but people will think they are, and trust me, that's the same thing.

Alex M H Smith
Author of No Bullsh*t Strategy
Founder of Basic Arts

Introduction

The Strategy Gap

Every year, without fail, executives and entrepreneurs gather in boardrooms and off-site retreats to dream up the future. With whiteboards covered in aspirational phrases and PowerPoint slides brimming with growth projections, they create visions that aren't just bold but revolutionary.

Yet, as time passes, many of these organizations find themselves mired in the same challenges, making marginal progress but never truly achieving the transformative change they envisioned. Teams drag their heels, and essential resources are directed to more immediate operational needs, all while the landscape your organization operates in is rapidly changing.

The result is stress and frustration. As the competition seems to be running circles around you, you find yourself making pragmatic decisions that deviate from the strategic vision and sabotage the potential impact of your bold plans.

It's almost like the vision was only a dream. A dream so rich in detail, so full of possibility, that upon waking you can still feel its power. Yet, as the day goes on, the clarity starts to fade, and by evening, all that remains is a vague memory…

In my career, I've witnessed companies around the world develop towering visions—visions that promised innovation, disruption, and paradigm shifts. They often sparkled with ambition, lit up boardrooms, resonated with potential, and dazzled stakeholders. But too often, these visions, no matter how bright, remained a distant dream that faded over time.

Why does this happen?

How do companies fail to realize visions that feel so vibrant and compelling?

The failure isn't in crafting the vision, but in aligning the thousands of daily business decisions towards it.

Every organization, whether they realize it or not, is an intricate web of decisions. The course of the organization isn't just shaped by a handful of boardroom resolutions, or high-stakes calls by the CEO, but by the sum of thousands of tiny choices made each day. Each team member, from the CEO making acquisitions to the intern creating slides, contributes to the journey. Ultimately, each choice, each action, collectively determines whether the ship sails smoothly towards its destination or veers off course.

This is where strategy comes in.

Strategy, at its core, is a commitment to how choices are made on your journey towards realizing your vision.

Together, these choices create a path. A path that keeps your business on track to making an impact.

If done right, strategy is much more than a high-level plan. It becomes the guiding light that aligns and empowers each member of your organization to make the right choices, steering the organization towards its desired destination.

But this is not a book about strategy.

It's a book about strategy *communication*.

Because surprisingly often, that's the missing link between vision and execution: effective strategy communication. The vision is strong, the strategy is smart, but outside the boardroom no one understands it or knows how to implement it.

Surprisingly few books guide leaders on how to do this. That's why this book exists: to help you communicate your strategy effectively so that you and your team know how to make the choices you need to make to progress towards realizing your vision.

Imagine your team turning from passive listeners into strategy ambassadors, not just understanding but championing your vision—and the rate of progress that makes possible.

Imagine meetings that are no longer about aligning misdirected efforts but about celebrating milestones and strategizing for new heights.

Imagine not racing against a clock set by competitors but setting the pace, confident in the knowledge that your team is right there with you.

This is the power of effective strategy communication. It turns the strategies you dream up into actions you see on the ground. The decisions you make are no longer reactive compromises but proactive steps towards a future you all embrace.

Over the past 16 years of working with leaders across the globe, I've distilled the PATH framework as a pragmatic tool to help organizations achieve this. It's essentially a checklist that helps you get your strategy communication right, identify holes in your communication, and even spot weaknesses in your strategy (so that you can fix them).

It's a simple framework with profound results.

At its core, PATH is an acronym that highlights four principles to turn strategy communication into a powerful decision-making tool. It stands for:

P: Plain and Simple—Do you speak a language that everyone in your organization understands?

A: Actionable—Do you make it obvious how decisions need to be made, even down to the tiny everyday decisions and actions?

T: Transformative—Do you encourage your team to make bold choices and challenge the status quo?

H: Heartfelt—Do you connect emotionally and spark a genuine passion for your collective journey?

In other words, do you light the PATH from your current reality to what you want your organization to become?

This book is your guide to unpacking and applying the four PATH principles. We'll look at examples from some of the world's biggest brands and how they lit their path to success. By contrasting successful companies that have used these principles to their fullest potential with those that stumbled, despite having a strong vision and a smart strategy on paper, you'll learn how effective communication turns your strategy into a powerful decision-making tool. The goal is to lead your team to wholeheartedly embrace the strategy, teach them how to make the right choices, and inspire them to make bold moves with conviction.

The book is structured into two parts.

Part 1 introduces you to the four PATH principles, starting with an overview (chapter 1) and then digging into each of the four principles in a dedicated chapter (chapters 2–5).

Part 2 explains how you can choose your own PATH (chapter 6), stay on track among complex organizational dynamics, market changes, and other challenges in your day-to-day operations (chapter 7), and finally how you can light the PATH and spread the word among your teams (chapter 8).

There's also an extensive list of checklists, case studies, and other resources on the book's website that will help you discover and implement the PATH principles in your own business. The self-assessment available there will help you see where your strategy communication is doing well and where it can lead to stronger outcomes and a more motivated team. You'll find everything at https://michaelgerharz.com/the-path/resources.

I highly recommend taking the self-assessment now so that you understand where you're coming from and then redoing it once you've refined your strategy communication using the PATH principles. It'll take less than five minutes, and I'll wait.

When you're back, let's discover the PATH to your strategic impact.

SCAN HERE for a quick 2 minute self test

Whether you're a startup trying to carve a niche, an established firm looking to reinvent, or simply a curious mind, let's embark on this journey. A journey from merely envisioning a destination to paving a clear PATH towards it—a PATH your organization will actually follow.

The PATH

Plain and Simple

Answer the simple question
"What is our strategy all about?"
in plain English!

Actionable

Make the right choice stand out
as if it were the only one!

Transformative

Encourage the team to make bold
choices with conviction!

Heartfelt

Find words that your team
truly believes in about the
things they deeply care about!

Impact

Part 1

Understanding Strategy Communication

1

The PATH to Strategic Impact

If you asked every member on your team what your strategy is and what it means for their everyday, how many of them could give a clear and compelling answer?

What if I asked you? Could you give that answer?

Strategy is supposed to be the masterplan, the grand design that sets your organization on a path to success, guiding every decision, aligning every effort, and charting a course to a triumphant future. But as we've seen, this idealized vision all too often crumbles under the weight of reality.

In the trenches of everyday business, strategy frequently becomes an enigmatic concept, shrouded in jargon, and confined within boardroom walls. Rather than serving as a clear guide, it turns into a source of confusion, with its messages lost in translation as they trickle down the organizational hierarchy. The gap between what strategy promises and what it delivers can be vast and disheartening.

This disconnect is not just a matter of poor planning or execution; it's fundamentally a communication breakdown. The way a strategy is conveyed determines how it's understood, embraced, and implemented at every level of the organization.

No matter how brilliant it is as a concept, a strategy can only be effective when it clearly resonates with those who are tasked with bringing it to life.

The failure to effectively communicate—and therefore execute—a strategy comes with both tangible and intangible costs. Resources are squandered on initiatives that don't align with the organizational vision, while time slips away with little to show for it. Perhaps even more damaging is the erosion of team morale, loss of employee engagement, and a culture marked by confusion and inertia.

Business history is packed with examples. Mobile phone manufacturers BlackBerry and Nokia struggled to find their path in a fast-changing world. Retailer Sears struggled with unclear strategies and, as a result, experienced chaos including disengaged employees and a deteriorating company culture. Yahoo's strategy was internally described as "spreading peanut butter across the myriad opportunities that continue to evolve in the online world" and changed a whopping 24 times in 24 years. Their inability to commit to how they want to make choices and effectively communicate a forward-thinking strategy caused team morale to tank and the business to lose against Google.

In each of these cases, the failure to light a path for the company manifested in lost opportunities, eroded market positions, and diminished brand value.

Wait! What Actually Is Strategy?

It might be time to take a step back and define what we actually mean by strategy. A good way to think about strategy is as a set of choices (often called a "plan") designed to help you achieve your goal (often to "win" in a game or a competition) under conditions of uncertainty.

A popular interpretation of this concept is the "grand masterplan" that a brilliant strategic thinker concocts alone in his office; his heroic effort will then defeat the competition in what feels like one fell swoop. But that's a rather romantic view of strategy. In fact, long gone are the days when strategy was synonymous with the solitary brilliance of a Napoleon at the helm.

A more modern approach to strategy recognizes it's no longer—and really never actually was—about a single leader figuring it all out. Instead, it's about empowering the entire team to be part of the strategic journey.

The truth is that trying to navigate your organization's complexity with only one driver is limiting and fraught with blind spots. It's much more appropriate to equip every member of your team with a map, a GPS, and the training to use them effectively.

This requires everyone to understand not just the destination, but also how their decisions and actions contribute to the journey towards that destination. This shift is profound—from a command-and-control model to a collaborate-and-empower mindset. As a leader, you light the path, but you trust your team to be able and willing to figure out how to travel it.

Tapping into the collective intelligence of the team leads to more innovative solutions, quicker adaptations to market changes, and a more resilient organization. Instead of having your team wait for directives from the top, you create an environment where the right choices can be made by the right person in the right place at the right time.

This is not to diminish the role of leadership in strategy. However, the leader's role shifts from being sole strategist to facilitator of strategic thinking across the organization. They create the pathways for information to flow, ensure goals align, and empower their teams with the tools and understanding to make strategic decisions.

Incorporating this modern approach into your strategy communication means moving away from top-down edicts and micromanagement. It means engaging in a dialogue, where feedback loops are constant, and every choice can refine and improve the strategic direction. It's about building a culture where the strategy is a living, evolving entity, co-created and owned by everyone in the organization.

By embracing this collaborative, inclusive approach to strategy, you harness the full potential of your team. You transform your organization into a fleet of informed navigators, each capable of steering their part of the fleet through the complexities of the business journey. The result is an organization that's not just led decisively forward but propelled by the collective strength and intelligence of its people.

With this in mind, strategy is not just about positioning or competitive advantage. It's about shaping the decision-making landscape of your organization. It's a commitment to a way of thinking, a cultural ethos, and a set of guiding principles that collectively drive the organization forward.

So we're not just looking at strategy as a plan or a set of choices pre-made by leadership. **Strategy is an organization-wide** commitment to how choices are made with the intention that every choice, big or small, propels the organization in the desired direction.

But that, of course, can only work when it's communicated effectively.

How Communication Can Ruin Strategy

When your strategy is unclear, your team won't know how to make the choices that need to be made. They'll end up being confused or simply following orders without understanding, if not giving up altogether. But even if the strategy is clear, when it lacks genuine commitment or passion, the team won't believe in the path and, as a result, won't be willing to walk the path, let alone make tough choices.

While it's tempting to pin the blame on external factors, the truth is that many organizations stumble due to internal lapses in strategic clarity (and, as a consequence, execution). The blame often lies in one of these common pitfalls:

> **Absence of strategy**: Surprisingly, some organizations operate without a strategy altogether. The vision is there, shining like a distant star, but there's no navigational chart guiding the ship towards it. In these organizations, decision-making often becomes reactionary, leaving them perpetually ill prepared for challenges and opportunities alike.
>
> **Fuzzy or unclear strategy**: For other organizations, strategy is little more than a gut feeling of the CEO. Teams are left to interpret random statements about the strategy, which often leads to misaligned initiatives or to plain misunderstanding

and confusion. The worst version is when these statements contradict one another or change frequently.

Fancy but intangible statements: Many organizations pay *marketing* agencies to craft fancy mission statements that sound poetic but offer little guidance. Beautifully worded and often replete with industry buzzwords, these statements end up as framed slogans on the wall rather than as actionable guides for decision-making.

Secret language: In other instances, the strategy is well thought out but written in a secret expert language only understood by a select few: the strategy consultants. It's made to make an impact but fails to do so because no one understands how to put it into action and what it means for the tiny everyday decisions they have to make.

The document dump: Finally, there are organizations where the strategy is buried in thick binders and long PowerPoint presentations that are seldom read, let alone understood or acted upon. It might as well be locked away in a vault for all the impact it has on daily choices and actions.

Here's the problem. When an organization's strategy fails to guide its myriad decisions—whether it's absent, ambiguous, impractical, or inaccessible—the vision, no matter how brilliant, cannot be realized.

Once you see this problem, it's obvious that great communication isn't optional, it's crucial. It becomes the foundational tool for shaping an environment where every team member's not just executing tasks, but making informed decisions that align with the strategic vision.

When the strategy is communicated in a language that everyone can understand, it demystifies the process of decision-making and turns executing the strategy into a collective journey. This clarity allows every team member to grasp not just the 'what' but the 'how' and the 'why' of strategic choices so they can make aligned decisions in their daily work.

Case Study: The Power of Alignment

Consider the story of Airbnb. In the early days, founders Brian Chesky, Joe Gebbia, and Nathan Blecharczyk saw a problem they thought they could solve: provide cheaper alternatives to hotels during high-demand events such as large conferences. Their idea to do this by making private space available was simple, but their path was anything but clear. Skepticism was rampant. Why would anyone allow strangers into their home? Why would travelers choose a stranger's living room over a safe hotel room?

The founders were determined to figure it out. They started by renting out air mattresses in their own apartment during a conference when hotels were fully booked. They built a website for others to do the same. When success wouldn't come, they visited their early customers—the hosts who would rent out spare beds in their apartments—to help them take better photographs and write better listings. They made many iterations to their platform, all while facing countless rejections.

But the real breakthrough came when they sought clarity about how they wanted to make choices as an organization—and got people on board with the resulting commitment to *creating a world where people could belong anywhere*. They turned it into a company-wide strategy that guided decision-making in all areas, from development to marketing, from customer experience to employee experience.

That's what allows a strategy to scale. When everyone in the organization understands how choices are made, the trajectory of the organization changes. Eventually, Airbnb became one of the largest players in the accommodation industry. Their revenue is now close to Hilton's.

The important lesson here is that Airbnb's rise wasn't (solely) due to the vision of its founders. To grow to that scale, a million choices had to be made along the way by thousands of people, from engineers to customer support to leadership. Aligning these choices along the "belong anywhere" credo is what allowed the company to innovate and adapt at scale—and to ultimately achieve its dream.

Crucially, it's not only a story about granting authority, it's about fostering a sense of ownership, alignment, and purpose. When each person feels that they hold a piece of the vision—when they see the path is as much theirs as it is the organization's—then the magic happens.

That's the impact great communication can have. When you find words that capture the essence of your idea, words that you truly believe in about the things you deeply care about, words that are not only plain and simple but also actionable, transformative, and heartfelt, that's when they inspire the people on your team to take decisive action.

It kept Airbnb from chasing a million opportunities in a thousand directions. Instead, they were making a million choices in *one* direction, focused on their strategy, which they communicated to the whole team, essentially with only two words: "Belong anywhere."

It's not *only* insight or *only* communication. It's both. You need the insight. And you need to find the words to communicate it effectively. But the communication is what's so commonly overlooked.

Great communication turns ambition into action and encourages bold moves. To achieve this, it must strip away the complexities and jargon that often shroud strategic directives and break them down into plain and simple terms that guide the entire organization. The PATH principles introduced throughout this book are designed to achieve that.

Let's look at one more example.

The Impact of a Clear PATH

When Tim Cook took the helm at Apple, he was stepping into the colossal shadow cast by Steve Jobs, a visionary leader known for transformative innovation. Cook, in his distinct leadership style, lit a path for Apple with a simple yet profound strategy: "Our goal has never been to make the most. It's always been to make the best." In an interview, he said: "Our North Star is making the best products that really enrich people's lives, and if we can't do those, we pass."

It's this standard that became Apple's compass, guiding every choice and action the company (and anyone in the company) would make. Communicating it clearly plays a major role in this. The compass isn't buried on page 43 of some complex strategy document written in consultant speak. It's a simple statement, in plain English.

Obviously, it has to be refined and made specific for each team. But, crucially, Cook's statement is concise and includes these refinements. It perfectly exemplifies the four PATH principles. Let's break it down:

> **It's plain and simple.** Every team member, whether they're in design, marketing, or customer service, understands their goal isn't just to sell more products or be the first to market, but to make the best products to enrich people's lives.
>
> **It's actionable.** When faced with a choice, the course of action becomes clear. For instance, should they add a feature that might compromise the user experience for the sake of ticking a box? Their strategy advises against it.
>
> **It's transformative** and has led to more than one revolutionary product. From the iPod to the iPhone to the iPad, they haven't always been first or market leaders, but they have often been the best. The strategy encouraged bold moves that, ultimately, not only transformed Apple but the entire tech landscape more than once.
>
> **Finally, it's heartfelt.** Apple's commitment to excellence is not just a corporate mandate, it's an ethos. It's a promise that every product released has been crafted with care and precision. If you work at Apple, it's very unlikely you're not passionate about these things.

What Apple's strategy communication exemplifies is the power of a clear commitment to how choices are made and communicating that effectively. Every choice, from the design of a new product to the layout of their stores, is filtered through the lens of their strategy. And please note: it's not just about what they choose to do; it's equally about what they choose not to do.

By finding words that made the strategy plain and simple, actionable, transformative, and heartfelt, Apple empowered its team to make choices that align with their broader vision. The strategy acts as a touchstone, guiding them through challenges and towards innovation.

A good strategy is a clear commitment to how choices are made in an organization. It turns into a *great strategy* when you can communicate it effectively so that everyone knows how to make those choices.

But how can *your* company, irrespective of size and industry, achieve that?

As we delve deeper into the subsequent chapters, we will uncover how you can light a PATH that leads to your vision, engages your team, and propels your organization forward. We'll look into each of the four principles, why they matter, and how they affect the impact—and ultimate success—of your strategy.

Turn the page to take the first step onto your new PATH.

2

P is for Plain and Simple
Understanding How to Make Choices

As much as we would like to believe in an easy way to success, that's not how it tends to work in real life. Organizations of more than a handful of people are inherently complex, with many balls to juggle, difficult decisions to make, and diverging interests to balance. On top of that, the world is changing fast, which turns business success into a moving target. Decisions need to be made swiftly despite incomplete information, competing interests, and uncertain outcomes, considering an arsenal of factors in ever-changing conditions.

Let's say it straight: The world of strategy can be messy.

But your communication should not reflect that mess.

You should be able to communicate—in plain and simple language—how choices are made in your organization. The choices themselves won't necessarily get easier. But to make them, you and your team need to understand what exactly the choices are and what guides them.

When you work in an organization that has no plain and simple way of saying how choices are made, it's as if you're handed a riddle rather than a clear set of tasks. The tools you need to do your job are scattered or missing, and the instructions, instead of helping, only create more questions. You look around, hoping for clarity, and see colleagues in the same boat—confused, frustrated, trying to decipher the next step.

It's like being given a puzzle without the picture on the box. You know (or at least hope) there's an end goal, but without clarity, it's difficult to know where to start, which piece goes where, or if you're even on the right track.

But when your communication states plainly and simply how choices are made:

1. **Every team member understands**: From the boardroom to the break room, everyone grasps the company's direction. There's no ambiguity, no room for misinterpretation.

2. **It's memorable**: People don't need to refer to a strategy document. It becomes part of the company lore, easily recalled and retold when needed.

3. **It's present**: It guides every decision, every action, in alignment with the company's overarching goals.

Let's first look at what this means outside of the office.

A Myriad of Choices in a Demanding Environment

When my children took their newly learned biking skills from the safety of our yard into the chaos of the streets, every turn, pedal, and pause bombarded them with choices to make. Stop or go at the crosswalk? Swerve for a shadow or stay straight? Extend their arm for a left turn or look over their shoulder? Wait at a parked car or bypass, with or without a hand signal? Ride on or give way at the intersection?

Every moment was a junction, every stretch a series of rapid-fire choices. To you, a mere bike ride. To them, a dizzying maze of incessant decisions in a high-stress setting not unlike a kaleidoscope—cars honking, pedestrians darting, lights blinking, and signs commanding. What a messy situation.

At some point, I asked my kids what they thought the rules in the street were for. A brief discussion ensued, which led them to realize that, basically, there's only one rule for biking: *Don't get killed!* Amidst the overwhelming cacophony of traffic rules, signs, and signals, that's the credo that binds all the individual rules together. "Don't get killed!" (We later suggested appending a second rule: "Be kind!")

It didn't necessarily make every choice easier. It wasn't a substitute for understanding the nuances of every traffic sign or the specifics of every turn. But it was a plain and simple way to capture the *spirit*, the underlying ethos. In every uncertain situation, this credo became the guiding principle, expressed in plain and simple language. Whether they were unsure about a turn, a sign, or an oncoming car, this clear and potent statement served as a touchstone for how to make the choice—the whole strategy for surviving in the streets captured in one simple statement. Everyone understands it. It's memorable. And it's present.

But wait, a myriad of choices in a demanding environment? Sounds very much like every day in business, doesn't it?

The Core Credo

Just like my children navigated the labyrinth of the city streets, businesses, too, find themselves in a whirlwind of decision-making daily. Product choices, marketing campaigns, sales calls, acquisitions, negotiations, interviews … the list is endless and the stream of incoming new choices never stops.

Amidst this hurricane of choices, how can an organization make sure their members understand how to make each one?

The same way my children did in the streets—with what I call a "Core Credo," a statement that everyone understands that's memorable and present.

A Core Credo can capture the very essence of how choices are made. It's not a detailed manual or a lengthy rule book. It's a succinct maxim that guides decision-making in our day-to-day work, be it the repetitive mundane tasks or—especially—the unfamiliar or complex situations that present us with new and unforeseen challenges.

The Core Credo is that one statement known and understood by everyone in the organization, easily memorable, and effortlessly shared. Its simplicity is not meant to replace the underlying complexity, but to make it accessible. The specifics of operational procedures, customer interactions, or product strategies remain crucial, but a plain and simple Core Credo can provide clarity, direction, and alignment. It's that signpost which, even when everything else seems uncertain or overwhelming, offers a clear reminder of the path we're on.

Case Study: Capturing the Spirit of the Strategy

Southwest Airlines, the Dallas-based low-cost carrier, offers a compelling example. First of all, their vision is very ambitious: "To be the world's most loved, most efficient, and most profitable airline."

But what sets Southwest apart is how they translated it into how choices are made. Part of their strategy is to maximize the time each plane spends in the air, because they realized that a plane only makes money when it's flying. The way they communicated that strategy from their early days on was brilliant: "Wheels Up." It's a simple Core Credo that captured the *spirit* of their strategy in just two words that are easily understood by anyone.

This simple statement informed decisions at all levels. For ground crew, it meant swift turnarounds at gates. For flight attendants, it meant streamlining onboarding service while still delivering their hallmark friendly customer service. For headquarters staff, it was about clearing bureaucratic obstacles. Everyone knew the strategy, and everyone knew their role in making it happen.

Just as "Don't get killed" emphasized safety above all for my children, "Wheels Up" crystallized Southwest's relentless pursuit of efficiency. To the uninitiated, it might seem like just another catchy corporate slogan. But for the Southwest team working in an industry rife with complexities and challenges, "Wheels Up" became the beacon that lit the path, simplified decision-making, and instilled a sense of shared purpose among all employees. The result? An airline that, despite the industry's notorious problems, consistently ranked at the top in customer satisfaction and profitability.

Now compare it to more common strategy wording. Southwest could have stated that their strategy was "to be at the forefront of efficiency." While that sounds spectacularly ambitious, it's also totally meaningless to most people in the business. It *looks* simple, but it isn't because the words are intangible and mean different things to different people. What does "efficient" really mean? How will you know you're at the "forefront"?

They could have refined it by stating that they want to achieve "60% airtime," but again, what does that mean for the staff or the cabin crew? It's a business metric that ground staff can't measure or make sense of.

They might, as their strategy, follow a very detailed set of rules. But that requires a huge amount of training and falls short in unforeseen situations. Southwest chose to empower their team in a plain and simple way instead.

They could have committed to doing "everything we can to minimize the turnaround time of our planes at the gate." But they figured that there was a much simpler way of saying the same thing, using only two words: "Wheels Up!" It's so plain and simple that everyone can understand what it means. It's memorable. And it's present. That's what makes it a Core Credo.

The Perfect Representative

A Core Credo serves as a compass, pointing towards the heart of the strategy and ensuring every decision aligns seamlessly with the organization's primary objective.

But a Core Credo does not, and should not, replace the intricate fabric of an organization's complete set of rules or strategic choices. It's not a shortcut to circumvent the established protocols, nor is it a one-size-fits-all solution. It doesn't replace the underlying complexity, it makes it accessible.

"Wheels up" echoes the essence of Southwest's operational efficiency, but behind those two words lies a robust framework of guidelines, procedures, and strategies. That framework helps Southwest operate well, but in decision-making moments employees look to the Core Credo for direction.

The beauty of a good Core Credo lies in its ability to evoke a vast knowledge reservoir. It acts as a mnemonic, a trigger that, when faced with a choice, helps individuals recall and align with the broader organizational principles and decision-making strategies. It reminds them of the path they're on.

In an ideal case, the Core Credo is a perfect representative of the underlying complexities of your strategy, understood by everyone and shared often so that it becomes deeply ingrained into the culture.

The cultural impact cannot be underestimated. In fact, I think this is the ultimate test of your Core Credo: Is it being shared? It's not hard to imagine "Wheels Up" being shouted between peers at the gate or being given as a short response in a meeting where different approaches are being discussed. It does have the potential to be shared. And that is profound. When everyone, from top to bottom, not only understands but *shares* a strategy, it becomes part of the company's DNA.

It's Not About Being Fancy.
It's About Being Clear.

This has nothing to do with fancy marketing slogans. In fact, it's not at all about being fancy. It's about being clear.

In the end, the only thing that matters is whether your team *gets your strategy*. Because, as we've seen, what use is a smart strategy when your people don't get it? So this whole chapter actually boils down to this simple truth: If they didn't get it, they didn't get it.

It's what I call rule number one in communication—and it's brutal. Your strategy may be smart but if your communication makes it feel complex, confusing, or meaningless, it can't have the desired impact. Which is not the team's fault. They don't get it because it isn't clear.

For instance, a company might announce a strategy to "leverage synergistic capabilities to enhance user-centric experiences." Sounds impressive, but how many team members know what "synergistic capabilities" are?

A government might announce a plan to "foster sustainable, inclusive growth through innovative policy measures." Again, sounds forward-thinking, but isn't clear at all.

A marketing consultancy might say their strategy is to "engage in holistic, multichannel brand elevation," but this sounds more like buzzword bingo than a practical plan.

And a startup, especially in its early stages, might pitch their strategy using high-level language like "disrupting the traditional industry model through a unique platform-based approach," but this is way too abstract for people to understand the practical application or feasibility of the business model.

In all these cases, the common thread is using fancy-sounding language that can mean all or nothing. It *sounds* simple but isn't because the words are vague. This vagueness can lead to misunderstandings, misaligned expectations, and, ultimately, failure to achieve the intended goals. To be effective, strategies need to be clear and specific.

Great communicators look tirelessly not for fancier but for *clearer* ways to say what they have to say. Their tool of choice is plain and simple language. And—in case it's not been clear until now—this applies not only to crafting a Core Credo but the *entire* strategy. What we've said about the Core Credo applies just as much to any other aspect of your strategy, down to specific rules or supporting material that explains the details. If they didn't get it, they didn't get it.

How to Find Plain and Simple Words for Your Strategy

For a select few, finding simple words is a natural talent. But the rest of us need to work hard to overcome the "Curse of Knowledge"—that strange phenomenon where the more we know about something, the harder it is to speak about that thing in simple terms.

Your best allies on that journey are the non-experts. That could be your friends, your customers, your parents or children, or even total strangers. Can you explain your strategy so that they understand it? Blank stares when they don't get what you mean will help you identify your weak spots. They'll tell you where you need to find simpler words.

Here's a list of questions that will help you find simpler words to communicate your strategy in a way that everyone on your team will get it:

1. **Distill the core**: Define the essence of your strategy. What's the one thing you want everyone to remember? Can you boil it down to one sentence (or less!) in plain English?

2. **Avoid jargon**: Speak in a language everyone understands. Omit industry buzzwords. Simplicity is key.

3. **Can you see it?** Because when you can, it means it's concrete. You can't see "60% airtime," but you can see "Wheels Up."

4. **Iterate and test**: Before rolling it out, test your strategy statement. Do people get it? Can they recall it a week later? Can they explain it to someone else?

5. **Embed it**: Make it part of your company training, onboarding processes, and, most importantly, regular communications. Reiterate and reinforce.

When you do this right, your strategy will get passed along. When people understand it and find it useful, they will pass it on to their peers and to the trainees and use it as a reminder when discussions heat up. Ultimately, *it nurtures culture*. Over time, your strategy will stop being just words. It will morph into your company's culture, guiding behaviors even when not explicitly stated.

Conclusion

Making your strategy plain and simple turns it into a flashlight in the dark. It shows everyone in the organization, not just upper management, where to step and where to avoid. It doesn't limit depth or ambition, nor does it complicate things. Instead, it makes them clearer and more accessible. When you light the PATH this way, everyone in the company knows what to aim for and how to get there.

While this is true for the entire strategy, the Core Credo in particular is a great way to capture the spirit of your strategy. Ideally, it's a perfect representative of the strategy that:

- conveys the essence of how choices are made
- guides decision-making, even in new and unfamiliar situations
- is understood by everyone in the organization
- is easily memorable
- is easily shared.

The capacity to be shared and travel through your organization is what helps your strategy become part of your DNA.

As we dive deeper into the other PATH principles, keep this in mind: Simplicity is the starting point from which all else flows.

3

A is for Actionable
Making the Right Choices Stand Out

Imagine a typical day at a software design studio. Let's call them "ETS—Elite Tech Solutions." We'll join Alex, the lead UI designer.

Alex leans back in his chair, staring intently at his computer screen. His team is responsible for revamping the main interface of the company's flagship software, a critical task for the new release. Alex has two design approaches in front of him. One is sleek and minimalist, reflecting the latest design trends. The other is packed with features and tools, showcasing the software's wide capabilities.

His brow furrows as he weighs up the options. ETS's credo is "to deliver exceptional user experience." Would the minimalist approach be seen as exceptional? Or does the feature-rich design, with its impressive capabilities, better represent that?

He convenes a team meeting to get input. The room quickly divides. Some argue "exceptional" means being ahead of design trends, hence supporting the minimalist approach. Others believe showcasing technological prowess is the way to go. The debate grows heated, the clock ticks on, and by the end, Alex feels even more confused and paralyzed by the choice.

This seemingly straightforward design decision is a microcosm of the bigger problem at ETS. Without a clear, actionable interpretation of their strategy, every choice becomes a potential point of contention. Every employee, from leaders like Alex to project managers and designers, feel the strain of trying to interpret what "exceptional user experience" truly means for their daily tasks.

Decisions that should be straightforward become mired in debate and second-guessing. Projects stall and teams grow frustrated.

The issue isn't the ambition of ETS's strategy but its ambiguity. The words used to communicate the strategy dilute the ambition rather than crystallizing it to give employees like Alex and his team a clear direction for their choices.

No one knows what a right choice looks like.

Therefore the strategy isn't actionable.

What Makes a Strategy Actionable?

When we speak of a strategy being "actionable," it's not enough to use plain and simple words. We're looking for an intuitive sense of what the right choice is in any given situation. The true value of an actionable strategy is in its ability to light the path so distinctly that choices don't just become easier—*they become obvious.*

The harsh truth is that a strategy that isn't actionable is, at its core, not a strategy at all. Without clarity on actions, it fails to fulfill its most basic purpose: to guide the choices that need to be made in your organization at every level every day. This risks a landscape of confusion, inefficiency, and lost opportunities.

Imagine for a moment that every decision in an organization is a switch that can be toggled on or off. An actionable strategy ideally ensures that, for every switch, there's an inherent understanding of which way to flick it so the choice aligns with the organization's goals and vision. No second-guessing. No room for prolonged debates. No room for ambiguity. The decision is almost automatic because the strategy has already laid the groundwork and pointed in the "right" direction for that choice.

Communication is, of course, essential here. The way you frame your strategy can make it either obscure or obvious how to act on it. Getting back to our example above, "deliver exceptional user experience" is obscure because it's unclear what that even means. What does it take to be "exceptional"? What does that look like?

A slightly better version would be to "design engaging UIs that empower users to accomplish tasks swiftly and seamlessly." That at least sets a focus on ease of use. But what's "engaging"?

Another version would be to "get out of your user's way to empower them to get the task done." Now it's obvious that fancy or trendy is secondary—getting the task done is primary.

An even more actionable and concrete version would be to "never require more than three clicks to get a task done." That's crystal clear in its intent and makes the right choices stand out.

Don't get me wrong, though. This is not the *only* way to make it actionable. Surely hundreds of alternatives exist depending on the actual intent; you might choose a different path for your company.

Regardless of the exact words you'd select, this is the role that effective communication plays: to bridge the gap from intent to action in an unambiguous manner. While the world of business can be complex, the decisions stemming from an actionable strategy should be stark in their clarity. It's the difference between sifting through a manual to find an answer and having that answer immediately pop into your mind, crystal clear.

Let's look at a real-world example.

Case Study: The Power of Obvious Choices

FedEx's early credo, "When it absolutely, positively has to be there overnight," wasn't just a catchy slogan. It was an embodiment of the principle we've just explored and a prime example of an actionable strategy.

Imagine being an employee at FedEx during its early days. You're faced with a challenging decision: A package has missed its scheduled flight. What do you do? Do you wait for the next flight, which is scheduled for tomorrow, or do you charter a new one? With a generic framing of their strategy, like "provide good shipping services," the answer's murky. But with "When it absolutely, positively has to be there overnight" ringing in your ears, the choice becomes intuitive, even obvious. The package needs to be there overnight, no compromises. Charter the flight!

This clarity wasn't reserved for extreme cases, either. Every touchpoint, from customer service to package handling, was informed by this mantra. Should a customer service representative spend an extra five minutes to make sure a customer's urgent package is delivered on time? Absolutely. Should the sorting team double-check packages slated for overnight delivery? Without a doubt.

FedEx's strategy communication eliminated ambiguity. It made priorities clear. Every employee, no matter their rank or role, knew what was expected of them. Choices often made themselves; there was no need for lengthy deliberations. Deliver it overnight, no matter what.

And the results? They spoke for themselves. In a logistics industry fraught with complexities and unforeseen challenges, FedEx emerged as a beacon of reliability. Customers didn't just use FedEx—they trusted them, implicitly. This trust wasn't built on marketing campaigns or sales pitches but the other way around. It was constructed, package by package, decision by decision, through the relentless, clear, actionable strategy that FedEx lived by every day.

This is the power of an actionable strategy. It simplifies complexity, aligns teams, and builds trust both internally and externally. By giving guidance on what "right choices" look like, it propels an organization forward, transforming vision into reality.

Once again, note that the strategy *became* actionable for FedEx through the *choice of words*. The same strategy could have been utterly inactionable if they had used generic statements or not bothered to capture the spirit of the strategy in a Core Credo. But they did bother.

The words they used made what could have been an abstract strategy concrete. They created an actionable strategy with the goal to remove doubt and make the right choice stand out, as if it were the only one.

But there's more nuance to this.

The Lazy Strategy: Concrete but not Actionable

Some companies define their strategy as a focus on an outcome, such as "double our revenue in the next five years."

It's a very concrete statement. But one that can be utterly frustrating, because you usually can't control it. When the CEO promotes it as the company's focus for the next five years, what does that mean for the team? How do they put it into action? It's not something anyone inside the company can *do*. Therefore, it's not actionable—and communication can't fix that.

An outcome-based strategy like this is what I like to call a "lazy strategy," which leaves the hard decisions fuzzy and vague. With a lazy strategy, it remains unclear how to act on it and what to do to make it happen.

Here's the crucial distinction: Actionable is not the same as concrete. "Double our revenue" is concrete but not actionable. It's only actionable when it's concrete about the *choices* that need to be made. If you delegate that to the team to figure out, you're being lazy.

Strategies are meant to *lead* to outcomes. But they are not *the* outcome. Instead, strategies need to guide the *actions* you take to achieve the outcome.

Therefore, a more helpful focus is one that informs actions and empowers decision-making within the team. This means capturing in words what a right choice looks like—the more concrete, the better.

In other words, actionable strategies are always concrete, but not everything that's concrete is actionable.

The Nuances of "Good Judgment"

But there's even more nuance to this. Because what's clear to you might not be clear to me and vice versa. To be actionable, your strategy needs to be concrete for *your* team, not mine.

A good example is the credo "Use good judgment in all situations," famously associated with luxury department store chain Nordstrom.

On the surface, asking employees to use "good judgment" seems neither concrete nor actionable. What does "good judgment" really mean? For one employee, it might mean prioritizing customer satisfaction, while for another, it might be about conserving resources. The ambiguity inherent in such a directive can be a challenge.

But Nordstrom, with its rich culture and history of exceptional customer service, has managed to give this directive profound depth. Through shared stories and examples, the company has painted a vivid picture of what "good judgment" looks like in practice. For example, in 1975, after having relocated to the site of a former tire store, they accepted and fully refunded a set of tires to a customer who returned them, despite the obvious confusion.

When a customer couldn't find the right size and color shoes at Nordstrom, the clerk, after checking other Nordstrom stores, found the right pair at Macy's, a competitor, and arranged for them to be shipped to the customer's home at Nordstrom's expense.

A third story is of a woman who lost the diamond from her wedding ring while shopping. Noticing her searching under clothes racks, a security staff member enlisted the help of two building services workers. They inspected the vacuum cleaner bags and successfully found the missing diamond.

Leaving a strategy as open-ended as "use good judgment" can be perilous. But through stories, Nordstrom gave an otherwise abstract statement concrete, actionable meaning. Naturally, though, these stories are unique to Nordstrom's ethos and built upon decades of consistent behavior and reinforcement.

The key takeaway here is not to mimic Nordstrom, but to recognize the importance of making your strategy actionable for *your* team. If your strategy involves a broad directive like "good judgment," it has to be clear so it's concrete and actionable for *them*. What do you mean by good judgment? In what context? What are some examples? Without these clarifications, employees are left to guess, which can lead to misalignments and inefficiencies.

Strategy, at its core, is not just about making *choices*, but about making the *right* choices—the ones that align with your strategic direction. The role of your communication is to be unambiguous about what "right" looks like for *your* company and for each member of *your* team.

How to Find Actionable Words to Communicate Your Strategy

The most important question to ask when you want your strategy to become actionable is this: Does it make the right choice obvious?

When your team can see what your strategy concretely means for their everyday actions, that's when your strategy turns from being words to being a guide. The role of communication is to bridge the gap from intent to action and find words that help you and your team see the right choice stand out.

This means looking for words that inform actions—rather than merely define outcomes—and that may involve sharing stories around your strategy. It's perfectly fine if outsiders don't get it, but it's non-negotiable that you make it clear for your team.

Here are several steps to help you find the right words:

1. **What outcomes do you aim for?** First circle back to your vision and the purpose behind your strategy. Why does your strategy exist? What are its goals? Understanding this will clarify what "right" looks like in situations that matter.

2. **Translate them into actions**: Identify what (kind of) actions are required. What can a team member *do* to make the outcome (more likely to) happen? What does the strategy look like when put into practice? It's not always as simple as FedEx's one-liner. But even if it isn't—especially then—the detailed specifics need to be just as clear and actionable.

3. **Illustrate with "how"**: Provide examples and scenarios that demonstrate how your strategy is executed successfully. This helps people visualize the actions they need to take, and it's what helped Nordstrom fill a generic statement like "good judgment" with a concrete, shared, and vivid understanding. Ideally, everyone on your team will be able to clearly describe in plain language what a right choice looks like.

4. **Solicit and use feedback**: Test your strategy communication with a diverse group from your

organization. Does it resonate with them? Is it understood and actionable? Ask them to recall some of their past decision-making challenges and share whether this new language would have helped make the choice easier. Refine it based on their feedback so it's practical and relatable.

5. **Embed and reinforce**: Integrate your strategy into the fabric of your organization, for example through using stories. Use it in training, decision-making frameworks, and as a regular part of dialogue in meetings. Consistent reinforcement turns strategy into habit.

When you do this right, it empowers your team to make choices that are aligned with your organization's core objectives, and creates a proactive and cohesive culture. The goal is to remove doubt and make the right choice stand out as if it were the only one.

Conclusion

Before we conclude this exploration of what "actionable" means for your strategy communication, let's go back to a fundamental idea introduced in the previous chapter: the Core Credo. Its plain and simple language lights the path ahead, but making it actionable magnifies the impact tenfold.

In other words, a Core Credo sets the direction, but it's the actionable unambiguity that provides the roadmap for each step of the journey. It guarantees your team not only knows the course but understands how to navigate it, even when the paths present them with unforeseen challenges and obstacles. By making the right choices intuitive and obvious, every member of the organization will be able to drive forward with confidence and cohesion.

And yet, we're still only halfway there. Understanding your strategy and establishing actionable unambiguity will serve your team well. But are team members actually willing to walk the path and leap ahead? In the next chapter, we delve into the "T" of PATH—transformative—to help you not only guide daily decisions but also inspire and instigate profound shifts in behavior, mindset, and results.

Onwards to transformation!

4

T is for Transformative
Encouraging Bold Choices

Strategy is often compared to chess. So let's imagine for a moment your organization's landscape is a chessboard. Each piece has a role and a set of rules for how to make moves. But in chess, you can't win *just* by following rules. The world's best players win because they know when to make the *bold* moves. It's what transforms their game from average to exceptional. It's what turns them from decent to grandmaster. And sometimes, it even transforms the game itself.

The transformative principle is about embracing this mindset across your entire organization.

Every morning, leaders and teams across your organization face a choice: to follow the well-trodden path of simply playing by the rules or to take a leap towards the extraordinary. It's easy for a team to get lost in the routine of safe decisions and incremental changes. These are the small steps that maintain the status quo, but they don't bring you decisively closer to realizing your grand vision. They don't provide that competitive edge that sets your organization apart from the competition.

The transformative principle challenges this. It's about recognizing that true innovation and strategic advantage don't arise from cautious steps but from decisive leaps. It's about seeing beyond the horizon of the familiar, no matter the size or scope of your organization. It's about daring to ask "what if" and then having the courage to pursue the answer.

Is your strategy communication that call to courageous action for the entire organization?

It's not enough for a strategy to be understood; it must be a catalyst for change, inspiring every team member to make bold choices. So how can you turn each decision, each project, and—yes—each team member into a potential game-changer? How can you shift the focus from reacting to the market to proactively shaping it?

The result will be profound. In an environment where transformative thinking is the *norm*, the mundane becomes a launchpad for the extraordinary. Every role, every task, carries the capacity for significant impact. This is where strategies evolve from being smart to being revolutionary, where the understanding of the shared path transforms into the collective drive to leap forward.

Let's look at how you can encourage your organization not just to understand the strategy but to make those bold, decisive choices that define the future.

Case Study: Making the Impossible Possible

When Paul O'Neill took over as CEO of aluminum producer Alcoa in 1987, the company was facing significant financial challenges. But, surprisingly to many, O'Neill didn't start with a focus on profit margins, production efficiency, or market expansion. Instead, he boldly declared: "I want to talk to you about worker safety. I intend to make Alcoa the safest company in America. I intend to go for zero injuries."

Perhaps the most astonishing aspect of this statement was that it was made in an industry synonymous with danger. Aluminum production, characterized by molten metal and heavy machinery, was responsible for many serious incidents. Alcoa, in particular, often wouldn't go a week in any of their plants without one. In the late 1980s, if someone suggested that aluminum plants could operate with zero incidents, it would have been dismissed as a daydream.

But for Alcoa, this "impossible" daydream became the cornerstone of their strategy.

To the investment community, it seemed an odd starting point. How would a strategy focused on worker safety boost revenue? But O'Neill understood something fundamental. He wasn't aiming only for safety. He was targeting a transformative change in company culture. If every employee believed that the company valued their well-being above everything else, it would instill a level of trust and cooperation that would spill over into every aspect of operations.

The results proved him right. It turned out that the focus on incidents was a vehicle to drive excellence throughout the organization. Within a year of O'Neill's leadership, Alcoa's profits had hit a record high. By the time he retired in 2000, the company's annual net income had multiplied fivefold.

A key aspect of this turnaround was O'Neill's framing of "zero incidents." Had he framed the safety strategy as "we want to improve worker safety," probably none of it would have happened. "Improve" encourages taking small steps, but "zero" calls for decisive leaps. "Improve" allows a lazy take of doing a little to check the boxes, while "zero" requires bold choices that lead to true transformation.

The Ripple Effect of Transformative Strategies

Alcoa's story underscores a crucial lesson: Transformative strategies have the power to catalyze systemic change. When an organization aligns to make a decisive leap that disrupts traditional thinking, the ripple effect extends far beyond the initial objective.

Alcoa's employees didn't just work safer. Their newfound sense of value and trust fostered a culture of innovation, collaboration, and excellence. Workers shared safety protocols, suggested process improvements, and felt empowered to voice concerns and ideas. The "zero incidents" Core Credo, though specific in its aim, became a benchmark against which every operation and decision was measured.

(Note how the zero injuries framing was not only transformative but also clear in its intent, making it both plain and simple as well as actionable. Such clarity in strategy communication meant every employee, regardless of their position, could understand, adopt, and promote this strategy in their daily tasks and interactions. It became a Core Credo that made the right choice obvious and a part of the company's DNA.)

Crafting and executing a transformative strategy is undeniably challenging. It requires the audacity to set lofty goals, persistence in the face of skepticism, and unwavering commitment to see it through. But the rewards, as seen with Alcoa, can be game-changing.

Not every company will have a transformative Core Credo as clear-cut as "zero incidents," but every organization can benefit from thinking in transformative terms. Whether it's purely internal or customer facing, about a shift in mindset or redefining customer service, about pioneering sustainable practices or reshaping an industry's landscape, transformative strategies lay the foundation for legendary success stories.

After all, the road to achieving bold visions is paved with choices that challenge the norm and dare to reimagine the possible.

If your team is willing to join you on the journey, that is. Enter JCPenney.

Case Study: No Transformation Without the Team

As the twenty-first century progressed, century-old American retail institution JCPenney found itself in troubled waters. Amidst declining sales and an outdated image, the company's leadership knew a turnaround was necessary. Ron Johnson was appointed as CEO in 2011 to achieve that. Johnson, who had previously garnered acclaim for his role in creating and leading Apple's retail strategy, arrived at JCPenney with bold visions for transforming the company.

His transformative ideas included:

- Eliminating sales and discounts, thereby replacing the company's long-standing high-low pricing model with a new "Every Day" low pricing strategy. He believed customers would prefer consistent and transparent pricing over the cycle of markdowns and sales.

- The Shop-in-Shop concept, to transform JCPenney stores into a collection of branded boutiques akin to a mini-mall.

- Getting rid of traditional cash registers and having employees check out customers anywhere in the store using iPads.

These ideas sound progressive on paper—and they certainly feel transformative (note the "Every Day" framing for low prices)—but they turned out to be a disaster for the company.

By April 2013, less than two years after Johnson's arrival, sales had plummeted by nearly 30%, and the company's stock price had dropped by over 50%. Johnson was ousted, and the company scrambled to revert to its old pricing model and appease its disenchanted customer base.

But what's the big difference between JCPenney and Alcoa? Both strategies were clearly transformational, yet only one worked. Well, first of all, it might have been the wrong strategy for JCPenney. We don't know. But one thing we do know is the effect the transformation had on the team.

JCPenney's transformation was done *to* the team, not *with* or *for* the team. All the choices had basically been made by upper management, and the team was expected to follow through with something they didn't even believe in. Many of them just didn't grasp the reasoning behind the drastic shifts, especially since some of the choices directly contradicted decades of the company's operational standards. They couldn't see how these were the right choices (despite being clear and actionable). They also found it challenging to justify them to the customers; the end of discount sales, a beloved JCPenney tradition, was a particularly hard sell. As a consequence, the team members didn't *want* to make those choices.

Alcoa's transformation was very different in this regard. It was about *encouraging* the team to make bold choices.

The lesson here is that for a strategy to be transformative, it's not enough to be ambitious or even disruptive *as a leader*. You need to spark that ambition *in the team*. If you can't get the team to join you in making leaps on your PATH, it won't matter how brilliant, bold, and transformative *you* are. The leaps won't happen.

At the heart of a transformative strategy lies the team's eagerness to make bold choices. This eagerness doesn't sprout from the mere understanding of the strategy's steps; it comes from a deep-seated *desire* to enact change. You need to tap into the team's collective ambition to not just participate in the journey, but to drive it. "Zero incidents" did that for Alcoa. "We use iPads for checkout" did not for JCPenney.

The aim is to incite a spirit within the team that craves innovation and impact. A spirit that looks at the horizon not as a distant dream, but as a driver for decisive steps forward. A force that compels each team member to not only make decisions, but to make them with hunger for progress.

How to Find Transformative Words for Your Strategy

The whole point of a strategy is to make *change* happen, to move you decisively closer to your vision. Being clear and actionable is not enough. You and your team need to be eager to make bold choices and take the leap. Are *you* eager to make them? Is your *team* eager to make them? Do you *encourage* them to make those choices?

The crucial question is therefore: What motivates your team to make the bold choices? That's the power of the "zero incidents" framing. It was as much the people's ambition as it was the leadership's.

Actually, it was more than that.

It took the ambition to the *extreme*—unlike, for example, "improve safety," which carries almost no ambition and therefore isn't transformative in spirit or scope.

When your strategy is expressed in language that lets the team see how their actions make a real difference, they will be much more invested in the idea of walking the path with you and making the deciding leaps.

Here are some suggestions and questions to help you figure out how to communicate your strategy so that it becomes transformative:

1. **Envision the impact**: Does your strategy not only detail the transformative change *you* seek, but also resonate on a personal level with *each team member*? Does it get people excited? Does it signal a shift from the mundane to the exceptional? Does it make each person feel that their contribution is a crucial part of something monumental?

2. **Challenge assumptions**: Empower your team to question the "we've always done it this way" mentality! Encourage individuals at all levels to think beyond the bounds of current practices and consider

what could be! What would "extreme" or "truly game-changing" look like?

3. **Foster ownership**: Frame your strategy as a collective endeavor. Invite input and grant everyone a stake in its outcome. When team members see their influence on the path, their desire to act on it and champion it will naturally increase.

4. **Set motivating ambitions**: Are your goals inherently motivating or just a boring follow-the-rules approach? Will your ambitions, when achieved, make everyone feel proud and excited, and tap into the intrinsic desire to be part of a success story?

5. **Embed transformation in behavior**: Beyond aligning with culture, your strategy must translate into behaviors that team members are eager to adopt. It should be framed in a way that making bold choices aligned with the strategy feels rewarding and fulfilling on both a group and an individual level.

By focusing on these elements, your strategy becomes more than a set of directives; it becomes a cause the team believes in and is eager to advance. The aim is to cultivate not just an understanding of what the *right* choices are, but a collective eagerness to make *bold* choices, driven by a shared will to make transformative leaps.

Conclusion

A transformative strategy stands as a bold declaration that the status quo is no longer enough. It's the deliberate choice to pursue a path less traveled, marked by the willingness to make decisions that are as strategic as they are symbolic. It's about turning the daily grind into daily growth, where the act of choosing becomes a reflection of the company's ambition and identity.

When your team leaps from *understanding* the choices to being eager to make *bold* choices, that's when you've arrived at a transformative strategy. Your strategy becomes the robust voice over the murmurs of hesitation, the firm hand that guides the team not only towards doing different things, but also towards doing things differently—with courage.

Consider this chapter an invitation to reject the seductive lull of the hamster wheel of just following the rules and doing it as it's always been done. Embrace the challenge of framing your strategy so that each decision is made with the intention to not just play the game, but to change it. That's the transformative spirit.

5

H is for Heartfelt
Getting Passionate About Your Choices

We have arrived at a point of the path where your team understands the strategy, sees the right choices stand out as if they were the only ones, and even dares to make bold moves.

But do they do it wholeheartedly? Do they fully embrace the strategy? Are they passionate about making it work?

This matters much more than some strategic "thinkers" would like to admit. After all, it's the humans in your organization who make your strategy work and, as humans, we're both rational *and* emotional.

When team members are emotionally invested, they're more likely to go the extra mile, persevere through challenges, and stay focused on long-term goals instead of short-term gains. They're more likely to support one another and work cohesively towards common objectives. And they're better equipped to handle setbacks, adapt to change, and overcome obstacles, as their engagement is rooted in passion rather than mere obligation.

In the end, *every* strategy, no matter how robust, will be tested by the heat of challenge and the weight of uncertainty. When the market turns against you, when the numbers don't add up, when team morale flags, that's the true test of your ambition. In these moments, a strategy must be more than a guide—it must be the shared heartbeat of your organization, offering hope amidst the pain and determination among the doubt.

Now imagine a path so aligned with who you are and what you stand for that it becomes a source of strength in these trying times. A path that gives a compelling answer to existential questions like "Why is that journey ours to undertake?" and "Why do we belong here?"

That's what the heartfelt principle is ultimately about. It underscores the necessity of embedding passion, shared values, and emotional resonance in a strategy, turning it into a unifying and motivating force within an organization.

In this chapter, we explore what happens when a strategy doesn't just speak to the mind but also resonates with the heart.

Case Study: Trusting the Team

In 2006, Jos de Blok turned the Dutch healthcare market on its head with a heartfelt conviction: We can trust nurses to know what's best for their patients. At his Buurtzorg community care organization, nurses work together in teams of 12 without a manager. Instead of having their work dictated to them, the nurses have enormous freedom in making decisions, big and small.

It's a revolutionary approach to healthcare, built on profound trust and heartfelt commitment to a simple idea about how choices should be made in healthcare: "Always start from the patient's perspective and prioritize their best interests."

De Blok believed that the individuals best positioned to make decisions in the best interest of the patients are those who directly interact with the patients. Where others bet on directives from the top, de Blok trusted each team member with feeling, understanding, and being passionate about the choices.

What's truly astonishing about the Buurtzorg model is how it contrasts sharply with traditional organizational structures. Other businesses lean heavily on centralized models and lay out a plethora of rules and detailed protocols to essentially force the team to make the right choices. To them, more rules means more control over the choices. Micromanaging is the result.

Buurtzorg, however, trusts the team *will* make the right choices if they *believe* in the choices. Fewer but *more heartfelt* rules are the result.

It has led Buurtzorg to achieve staggering results. The company boasts the highest satisfaction rates among any healthcare organization in the Netherlands—a testament to the efficacy and resonance of their approach. Moreover, while ensuring premium care for its patients, Buurtzorg has simultaneously brought about significant financial efficiency. A KPMG study has found that if all home care in the Netherlands was provided using Buurtzorg's model, it could save the Dutch healthcare system around 40 percent.

But make no mistake! That was only possible because de Blok precisely captured what drives the team: caring for patients! Their nurses don't show up to follow a corporate mandate; they engage in a mission they deeply believe in. Caring for patients is why they applied for the job in the first place. Now, every day, they're reminded of the difference they make in their patients' lives, and this acts as a continual source of motivation.

Pay attention to what a difference the wording makes. Buurtzorg's strategy wasn't to "provide effective healthcare at a reasonable price," it was to "always start from the patient's perspective and prioritize their best interests." The former is what businesses might care for; the latter is what nurses care for. It speaks to their heart. At the same time, it's plain and simple (expressed in plain language), actionable (it's clear you should do what's best for the patient), and transformative (because the healthcare industry used to work under a very different paradigm).

But there's even more to it when you find words your team truly believes in about the things they deeply care about. The heartfelt principle ensures the communicated approach isn't just a passing trend or a catchy phrase. If done with empathy for what matters to your team, it positions your strategy as a deep-seated commitment that motivates the team to push forward, even when faced with setbacks.

Let's get a little deeper into this.

The Sustainable Fuel: Passion and Commitment

Imagine a transformative strategy that demands significant changes, tough choices, and relentless effort. If the team doesn't genuinely believe in it—if they're not deeply passionate about the choices—they might begin to question their path when faced with inevitable hurdles. Without that heartfelt conviction, it's all too easy for individuals to lose interest or even give up, asking themselves, "Is all this effort truly justified?"

The worst outcome might be when this leads to a mindset of indifference. If team members aren't genuinely connected to or invested in the path, they might detach and think "Not my job."

And that's exactly what so often happens with a lazy strategy that isn't heartfelt:

- The 10% growth isn't met? So what, asks the team member down the line.

- Follow the rules? Sure, that's what I'll do. But no more than that.

- An unforeseen event? Not my job! Let the boss deal with it!

On the flip side, when a strategy is genuinely heartfelt, it becomes a source of intrinsic motivation. "10% growth" turns into "the patient's best interest," something the team deeply cares for. Business-wide rules align with personal values. Unforeseen events get dealt with directly because it matters to the team member personally.

It's no longer just about fulfilling a role or ticking off boxes; it's about being part of a larger purpose, something that resonates deeply with individual values and aspirations.

This is what propels teams not only through the good times but especially through the toughest challenges. It ensures they stick to the path and do so with unwavering dedication and vigor.

The Power of Identification

I will even go so far as to say that a strategy carried by conviction doesn't just define a path. It crafts an identity.

It's not about competitive positioning or market share anymore; it's about the soul of the organization. A heartfelt strategy articulates why *this team*, with *these people*, is embarking on *this particular journey* together. In a way, it's the answer to the fundamental questions of "Why?" and "Why us?"

With a heartfelt strategy, these questions are answered in every patient visit by a Buurtzorg nurse, in every package delivered by a FedEx driver, on every Southwest Airlines plane that takes off. It's answered when the daily work reflects personal values and contributes to a narrative larger than the sum of its parts. It's in these moments that employees are not merely participants in a process but protagonists in a story they perceive as meaningful.

But this story doesn't emerge by chance. It's the result of deliberate cultivation—words intentionally chosen to intertwine with the team's passions and motivations. This turns your strategy into an ethos, a theory of what's right not only from a business perspective but from a human perspective. After all, a company isn't just a business entity; it's a collective of human endeavors, aspirations, and yearnings for impact.

By connecting the company's narrative with the personal stories of its team members, a heartfelt strategy ensures that "Why?" and "Why us?" are answered not only in a single moment, but in the ongoing journey of the organization—a journey that each person helps shape every day with the work they do, the decisions they make, and the passion they bring to their roles.

Most strategies are about the what, but the best strategies answer the why, too—at least implicitly. For this to happen, you need to peel back the layers of corporate financial goals to reveal the core values and passions that drive the organization and uncover the collective narrative that says: "We're not just here to work;

we're here to make a difference, to contribute to a story in which we all believe."

Your strategy gets shared because it's plain and simple. It guides decision-making because it's actionable. It motivates because it's transformative.

But it *endures* because it's heartfelt and matters on a personal level.

How to Find Heartfelt Words to Communicate Your Strategy

How you articulate a heartfelt strategy can be the difference between a plan that sits on a shelf and one that lives in the heart of every team member. Communicating in a way that fosters a deep connection requires not just clarity, but also empathy and authenticity.

We've seen many examples throughout the book. "Zero incidents" was deeply heartfelt for Alcoa's team. It meant they were safe at work—especially meaningful when the opposite was usually true. A different version of the same strategy articulated from a purely financial perspective, such as "Reduce costs for incident care to zero," would almost certainly not have been heartfelt, even though it's basically the same strategy.

Or think about Airbnb. "Belong anywhere" feels very different than "Make the world's spare bedrooms accessible." Both versions are plain and simple, actionable, and transformative. But only one is heartfelt. The second one asks "What makes sense for the business?" The first one asks "What makes sense for the humans that run the business?" (Note how it also asks "What makes sense for the customer?")

Here are some thoughts to help you find words that create a heartfelt connection:

1. **Listen**: Have open conversations with your team to understand what matters to them. Why did they sign up for the work? What are their personal motivations and drivers?

2. **Speak to the heart**: Use language that transcends the transactional aspects of business. Communicate in a way that speaks to the aspirations and values of your team, using narratives that connect daily tasks to the greater purpose they serve.

3. **Invoke a shared purpose**: Highlight the common ground that unites your team—shared goals, shared struggles, shared triumphs. Use storytelling to reinforce the sense that everyone is part of a larger journey.

4. **Personalize the message**: It can be very helpful to refine the strategy for different parts of the business to make the team's contribution more personal. Tailor your communication to reflect the diverse roles within your team, illustrating how each contributes to the overarching strategy. Make it clear how individual efforts are integral to the collective mission.

5. **Express authenticity**: Be genuine in your communication. Identify and share why you, the leader, care. If a strategy comes from the heart of the leadership, it will resonate more deeply with the team. Authenticity breeds trust, and trust lays

the foundation for heartfelt engagement. Does your language reflect that? Or is it dry, corporate, and distanced?

6. **Encourage dialogue**: Foster an environment where feedback is not just accepted, but welcomed. Open dialogue ensures the strategy is understood and embraced, and it allows team members to express how the strategy resonates with them personally.

By focusing on these communicative approaches, the strategy becomes more than instructions: it becomes a shared belief. The right words can inspire, motivate, and comfort, turning strategy communication into the thread that weaves the fabric of a united, purpose-driven team.

Conclusion

And so we arrive at the heart of the matter. A strategy that endures is one that is felt deeply. It guides through the good times but also when the numbers don't quite add up, when the market shifts beneath our feet, and when the easy thing to do isn't the right thing to do.

The genuine passion for your collective mission lights the path, not just for the mind to follow, but for the heart to lead. With every choice made, every challenge embraced, and every triumph celebrated, it answers the soul-searching question of "Why us?"

As we wrap up the four PATH principles—Plain and Simple, Actionable, Transformative, Heartfelt—we see that it's more than a methodology: it's a manifesto. It's a commitment to not only make strategies that are easy to grasp, practical to implement, and bold in ambition, but also to imbue them with the kind of sincerity that can weather any storm.

That's my call to action for you: to build strategies that resonate with your team not just on the surface but at the core, to communicate not just with clarity but with authenticity, to lead not just with vision but with empathy!

Let your words light the PATH your team wants to walk, not out of obligation, but out of desire. Not to the finish line, but towards a horizon that keeps expanding as you approach it...

Part 2

Applying the PATH Approach in Your Organization

6

Choosing Your PATH

By now, you'll have seen how the PATH framework can help you and your team make the right choices with courage and conviction. But you may also find yourself at a crossroads, inspired and motivated, yet wondering, "How do I make this work in my unique organizational landscape?"

In the following chapters, we'll look at three crucial areas:

1. How to choose your PATH (this chapter).

2. How to navigate the obstacles that may arise while you're on your PATH so you can stay on track (chapter 7).

3. How to light the PATH by inspiring and motivating your whole team to join you on the journey (chapter 8).

The beauty of the PATH framework is that it carries the answers to these questions in its very core.

We've seen how strategy is essentially a commitment to how you want to make choices. Let's start with the biggest choice of all: choosing the PATH itself.

As much as we would like it otherwise, figuring out the right strategy is often a colossal task. It involves insight and intuition, observation and opinion, forecast and foresight. It's a blend of subjective judgments and objective analysis. A dance between what is and what could be. You need to connect dots in seemingly random patterns, discern trends from the trivial, and project possibilities from the present. On top of that, you need to be able to articulate what you've discovered in a clear and concise manner so that it can be acted upon.

Here's how most organizations do it (and I think it's a mistake): First, they spend months doing analysis in a more or less rigorous process. *Afterwards*, they look for ways to communicate the outcome of that analysis—only to discover it hasn't quite worked out as expected. Their strategy *can't* easily be put into words. It's too complex, confusing even, and people are left wondering what it means for their everyday.

As a consequence, choices on every level keep being made in an ad hoc fashion and are scattered in many directions—the opposite of confidently moving in one strategic direction. All the while, new opportunities pop up and attractive ideas emerge, which makes leadership think they need, well, a *new* strategy. And so the cycle continues for another loop.

But some of the world's most successful organizations do it a little differently. They realize that figuring out a strategy is as much about *finding the right words* as it is about doing rigorous analysis. They understand that caring about the words they use can help them see their PATH more clearly—from the very first steps—and make better choices as a result.

Let's look at an example.

Finding the Courage to Focus and Amplify

Duracell is one of the world's largest battery manufacturers. They have a huge product range. But everything they do, including every single piece of communication, boils down to the core value of wanting to be known for durability. Their promise is that Duracell batteries keep running when other batteries have long given up. It's even in their name: *Dura*ble *cell*.

By committing to one core brand promise and sticking to it for decades, Duracell got the clarity around making choices that allowed them to scale significantly and become known for that brand promise.

This was almost certainly a deliberate act. They *chose* to ignore all the other possible promises—such as cheapest or most innovative—and stick with durability, as exemplified by their famous pink bunny (except for in the United States where, due to a weird brand battle with Energizer, the pink bunny is being used by the latter). It's easy to see from the outside how well this sustained focus has worked for Duracell.

But of course, when it's about us, things are a little different. Fear of focus kicks in—we feel we can't just commit to one path because this path to the right is worth exploring as well, we've heard fascinating reports about the breathtaking view from that path to the left, and we have these 15 ideas, 23 products, and 41 customer requests to take into account.

And so we lose focus on both our actions and our communication. Instead of a clear, guiding path, we pursue a plethora of small routes in all sorts of different directions, making little progress in each rather than massive leaps in one.

Which makes our work harder than it should be, on multiple levels. It's hard to decide which tasks are important and which are not. It's hard to tell a concise story about our project. And it's hard to find a plain and simple way to explain how we want to make choices.

Which of the 13 important projects do we prioritize this month, this week, or today? Which one gets the spotlight on our website? Or in our press coverage? What do we say to the customer on the phone? Or to our business partner in a meeting?

Here's the thing: If *you* don't decide on what matters most in your strategy—if *you* don't pick a focus—you're basically delegating that decision to your team, to your customers, and to time. You're letting *them* do the hard part of choosing the focus.

You might not be too happy with their choice.

Or you might find that not much is happening in the business at all.

Focus is hard, no doubt about it. If you're passionate about what you do, there will always be more interesting things to do than you've got time for. Yet, if you don't make the choice early, you're going to battle it out later, at a time when potentially every choice has become a struggle because you've invested energy and resources into doing them all even though you can't.

So make that one choice early to replace the thousand choices later. What's the essence of your strategy? What's the core choice you make in your organization *at the start* that determines how you make the subsequent smaller choices on the journey?

That's where the Core Credo comes in. It's a great tool to help you make that crucial initial choice.

I suggest you look at it like this: If you can't summarize the essence of your strategy with a plain and simple Core Credo, it's very likely that your strategy is too complex and your team members will fail to see the strategic direction.

As I said in the introduction, a great way to think about the PATH principles is as a checklist. This is the first—and perhaps the most important—check: Can you capture the spirit of your strategy in a Core Credo?

In that sense, choosing your PATH means stripping away anything that's non-essential and amplifying the essential, much like Duracell, whose batteries "keep running when other batteries have long given up." It's not the whole of their strategy but it captures the spirit—a spirit they chose, focused on, and amplified decisively. Focus and amplify!

In the same way, the other PATH principles help you identify appropriate strategic choices before fully committing to your strategy. When you're sitting through presentations in a strategy meeting and need to draw conclusions, the PATH principles will help you figure out early which approach has the potential to inspire your team:

- Is this something everyone in our organization knows how to put into action?

- Does this encourage bold choices that have the potential to transform our organization or even our industry?

- Is this a shared passion that leads everyone to wholeheartedly embrace our strategy?

When you can articulate compelling answers to these questions in plain and simple language that everyone in your organization understands, then you might be onto something. The earlier you ask these questions, the more directed the process will become.

That's the lesson here: PATH offers you a set of questions to ask. If you answer them rigorously, you'll not only end up finding better words, you'll also end up understanding your strategy better. Is it plain and simple? Is it actionable? Transformative? Heartfelt? That, in my experience, is what sets the best leaders apart. It's not that they have all the answers. It's that they know which questions to ask.

And they keep asking them until they get it right.

The Path to Getting it Right

Obviously, your PATH won't be a one-time revelation, let alone a sudden stroke of insight. Boom! Here's focus and clarity.

It's much more likely to be a process of continuous refinement.

Think of Dyson, who famously went through 5,127 prototypes of his vacuum cleaner in a relentless commitment to excellence. Although the final design looks strikingly simple, the process wasn't by any measure. But being clear on how to choose the good designs from the bad was a deciding factor in a journey on which being right initially mattered less than getting it right eventually.

For your strategy, it's the same. The truth is that the path to strategic clarity is rarely linear. It's a cycle of trial and error, feedback and refinement. Your first attempt's probably not going to nail it. But what first attempt ever does?

The good news is that the PATH principles help you refine it until you do get it right.

The most important step is to start *somewhere*. Make a first attempt at articulating your strategy. It literally doesn't matter whether it's any good, as long as you write it down. When it's on paper, the PATH principles will immediately jump in to help you evaluate it and guide you towards getting it right. Just keep asking the questions: Is it plain and simple? Is it actionable? Transformative? Heartfelt?

This commitment to continuous refinement fuels the leap from good to great organizations. It's absolutely not about being right *at the first step*, but about getting it right *in the long run*.

Almost none of the examples in this book got it right initially. It's not that the CEO simply had that sudden stroke of genius. The compelling strategies we see in the real world are overwhelmingly the result of continuous refinement, driven by the will to get them right. It takes the greatest companies years to arrive at a strategy that works. Read Jim Collins's famous book *Good to Great* for proof.

I won't promise you otherwise. PATH is not meant as a quick fix for your urgent strategy problem (although it can be a useful diagnostic). It's a tool you can (and should) come back to, whenever things have shifted or something doesn't feel quite right. Encourage your team to view each step as an opportunity for improvement and learning rather than a final verdict on success or failure. Implement a system of regular review and feedback for your PATH. Challenge your team to be candid in their assessments and open to revisions so that, over time, it evolves to meet the true essence of your vision.

Let me stress this again: Strategic choices are often inherently complex. The commitment to a PATH is not meant to dumb this complexity down by pretending that all you need to do is come up with a simple-*sounding* Core Credo. Quite the opposite. The point is to make the complexity *accessible*, to find a way that *guides* you through the complex mess of a business's everyday life. It's through the simple words that we make the complex thoughts and choices achievable. It's through plain and simple language that, eventually, we get it right. Simplicity is not the opposite of complexity: it's the prerequisite.

Tapping into Your Team's Brilliance

But there's one more important lesson here: Leadership doesn't have to be the sole bearer of wisdom. In fact, such a notion can be a considerable roadblock.

Your perspective, no matter how seasoned or insightful, has limits. There's a universe of ideas, insights, and innovations residing within your team. Their on-the-ground experiences, diverse viewpoints, and unique skills are invaluable in choosing and shaping a robust PATH.

Scott Kelly, former commander of the International Space Station, sums this up nicely: "The smartest person in the room, I've learned, is usually the person who knows how to tap into the intelligence of every person in the room." Leaders are effective not because they know, but because they *want* to know. We trust them not because they have the one and only answer, but because they have the will to find the best answer—whether that's their own or a junior's.

Your first task is to create channels where ideas can flow freely. This means fostering an environment where every voice is not only heard, but valued. From the quietest intern to the most outspoken senior manager, encourage a culture of sharing and collaboration.

In meetings, don't just rely on the loudest voices or the most senior positions. Seek out those who are often overlooked. Ask the assistant, the quiet analyst, the new hire: "What's your perspective? What could we be overlooking?" This isn't about being democratic for the sake of it; it's about recognizing that the most valuable insights often come from unexpected sources.

When you go through the hassle of sifting through the wealth of insights and let the PATH principles guide you, you'll be able to find the golden threads that align with your PATH.

A strategy shaped by a single mind can be strong, but one forged by the collective intelligence of a team is resilient. It's adaptive, multifaceted, and grounded in a broader understanding of the challenges and opportunities your organization faces.

Take a page from Pixar's playbook. Their Braintrust approach, where diverse groups provide candid feedback on projects, has been pivotal in creating some of the most successful films. It's not about consensus, but about harnessing diverse perspectives to refine and elevate ideas.

Finally, encourage your team to take risks with their ideas. Make it known that insight is rewarded, even if it challenges the status quo. Create an atmosphere where obvious isn't the default, but rigorous and insightful are. Cultivate a culture where every perspective is valued. Make it clear that, in your team, titles don't dictate the value of an idea. Encourage a mindset where questions like "What do you think?" become the norm, not the exception.

By tapping into your team's brilliance, you don't just gather ideas, you weave a tapestry of collective insight. It's a strategy enriched by the experiences and perspectives of every team member. As a leader, you're the catalyst for this symphony of ideas, guiding and harmonizing them into a PATH that's as robust as it is dynamic.

Your PATH Awaits

Choosing your PATH is a transformative expedition that reshapes your organization into a strategic powerhouse. If you get it right, you will empower every member of your team to make choices that align with your collective vision. The idea of your strategy is just as important as the words you use to communicate it. Both have tremendous influence on how you travel, the choices you make, the lives you touch, and the legacy you build.

If you choose wisely and lead passionately, every step on this PATH will be a stride towards a future that is as bright and promising as the vision that guides you.

Therefore, resist the temptation of the first idea and the quick fix. Take your time and let the PATH principles guide you. Use it as a checklist from the very first steps of your strategic process until you get it right. When you find the right words to bring your strategy to life, they will transform intent into action so each decision, no matter how small, contributes to your organization's journey.

7

Navigating Your PATH

On your journey of implementing the PATH framework, you will inevitably encounter a myriad of obstacles.

You strive to keep your strategy plain and simple, but in the boardroom, where shareholder demands and market pressures collide, simplicity is often the first casualty. You're under pressure to expand, diversify, react to every market tremor—but each reactive shift clouds your strategic vision, obscuring the clear PATH to light.

As you navigate internal politics, the goal of keeping strategies actionable becomes entangled in a web of conflicting agendas. The clarity of action you aim to instill is lost in translation, diluted by the undercurrents of power play and departmental rivalries. Your vision of a united, forward-moving organization seems like a mirage in a desert of political maneuvering.

In your efforts to make your strategies transformative, you confront the formidable wall of organizational inertia. Each step towards transformation is met with resistance, a resistance born out of fear, uncertainty, or simply the comfort of the status quo. You find yourself not only charting the path but also having to clear it, like you're pushing against an immovable object.

Perhaps most challenging is ensuring your strategies remain heartfelt in an environment that often prioritizes profit over people. In the face of cold, hard numbers and bottom-line thinking, keeping the human element at the heart of your decisions is a constant battle. You know that for your PATH to be truly effective, it must resonate with every member of your organization, yet in the daily grind, this connection can feel tenuous, almost slipping through your fingers.

In this high-stress, high-stakes scenario, your endeavor to light a clear PATH might feel like navigating a ship through a stormy night, with only a flickering lantern to guide you. The gusts of competing interests, the waves of internal politics, and the pressure of market forces threaten to extinguish this light at every turn.

But I'd like to encourage you to reframe these challenges as opportunities to strengthen and refine your strategic approach. Ultimately, the roadblocks are just features of the overall terrain. This section is dedicated to navigating these obstacles so the PATH you set forth remains clear and navigable, even in turbulent times.

Navigating Complex Organizational Dynamics

In an environment where agendas and priorities frequently clash, conflicts are inevitable, even more so when the debate is over the strategic PATH that's influencing the direction of the entire organization.

Take the apparel company that's considering expanding its market presence into a new continent with different cultural and fashion sensibilities. The Sales Director's enthusiastic about the potential for revenue growth, but the COO's hesitant due to the logistical challenges, the need for a local workforce, and the adaptation required for product lines to meet local tastes.

Or the multinational corporation that's discussing implementing a new corporate social responsibility initiative to reduce its carbon footprint. The CMO sees it as an opportunity to enhance the brand's appeal to a growing market of environmentally conscious consumers, but other executives think the funds could be better used for immediate profit-generating projects.

Navigating steadily through these conflicts often comes down to three core ideas.

Defining Who You Want to Be

The natural inclination when facing conflict or resistance is to ask: "What's wrong with them?" Perhaps the Sales Director thinks the COO is a coward, and the COO thinks the Sales Director is risking the business. But this thinking will lead you down a path of blame and deadlock when—considering these are smart people—there are quite likely excellent reasons on either side of the argument.

That's why I suggest a different perspective: It's not about who *is right*. It's about *who you want to be* and *where you want to go* as a team. The easy way out might be to sidestep conflict, hoping it'll resolve itself. But more often than not, this results in even deeper fissures down the road. It's way more useful to face it straight on, as conflict is precisely the kind of conversation that will lead you to your true values and fill your strategy with meaning—much like Nordstrom in chapter 3. Certainly, "use good judgement" was the fuel for many heated discussions in many meetings.

We'll reach better solutions if we assume there's a good reason for the other side's stance. Asking "What's going on here?" in place of "What's wrong with them?" opens a window to understanding the root causes of conflict and misalignment. It leads to a joint effort to *get it right* rather than a fight over who *is* right. The choices you make from these conversations will define who you truly want to be.

It won't guarantee immediate resolution, but it will start the process of untangling the knots.

Enforcing Clarity in Communication

Clarity is your ally in this terrain. Too much time is wasted in discussions over unclear terminology, fuzzy concepts, and misaligned understanding.

It starts with simple things like "$5 million." Is that a lot or not? And vice versa: When you say "a lot," how much are we talking about, really?

The CTO hears "efficiency" differently than the CFO. And in the meeting about a new product launch, different departments might bring very different concerns, all of which make sense when you look from their perspectives. Sales is worried about targets, Marketing about the campaign aligning with the brand values, and R&D about the technical feasibility.

To make matters worse, everyone's using their own terminology, and some team members shy away from making concrete statements, hiding behind general but abstract observations or objections.

But it's hard to make choices when you can't even be sure what the choice is *exactly*. So that must come first. In meetings, team interactions, and conversations, enforce clarity in both speaking and listening. If you, as the leader, don't settle for confusing communication, your team won't either.

The best question to ask when you want to speak with clarity is "Can you see it?" Because when you can see it, it means it's concrete. For example, you can see "Wheels Up", but you can't see "60% airtime." You can see a packet being delivered overnight, but you can't see "efficient delivery."

Try pushing your team to use simpler words whenever someone (really, anyone!) doesn't understand something. Ask them to use simpler visuals that show exactly what they want them to show. And sometimes, you might even have to force them to go back to the drawing board and find those simpler words rather than having the listener figure it out for them. As journalist Wolf Schneider famously said, "Someone's got to suffer, either the reader or the writer."

Yes, it might slow things down in the beginning. But the clarity and acceleration you'll experience down the road will compensate for that many times over. So encourage a culture where team members feel comfortable asking for clarification, value feedback on their communication, and apply the standards of active listening. When teams pivot to a communication style that is plain and simple, the fog begins to lift, the choices come into plain sight, and the conversations focus on what's really at stake.

Clear communication removes ambiguity. It surfaces misalignments and brings to light areas where the organization's actions are not in sync with its goals. Employees can move from working in silos that defend their perspective to engaging in cross-functional dialogues, breaking down barriers, and building bridges of cooperation.

Parting Ways

But there's one caveat. Seeing the path clearly doesn't necessarily mean it's for everyone. This clarity, while unifying, can also light divergent paths—and that's perfectly okay.

In the pursuit of our strategic goals, it's essential to understand that alignment isn't just about marching forward together; it's about ensuring everyone is on the same path willingly and wholeheartedly. The PATH framework is not just a tool for navigation; it's a litmus test for commitment.

As leaders, our role is to articulate this PATH with such clarity that it leaves no room for ambiguity about what the journey entails and what is expected of each member. This clarity will, in turn, enable every individual to make an informed choice: to walk this path with us or to find a new one that aligns better with their aspirations and values.

It's important to approach this juncture with empathy and respect. Those who find their paths diverging from ours are not adversaries; they are colleagues who have shared part of the journey with us. In acknowledging this, we part ways with gratitude for the distance traveled together and with good wishes for the paths they choose to pursue.

This moment of parting is not a failure but a natural progression in the life cycle of any dynamic organization. It's a sign of a healthy environment where choices are respected, and personal and organizational growth are valued equally. By allowing for these divergent paths, we foster a culture of authenticity and integrity.

As we continue on our path, let's remember that the strength of our journey lies not just in the steps we take together, but also in the grace with which we respect and honor the steps taken in different directions. Our vision is clear, the path is set, and as we move forward, we do so with the understanding that this journey is for those who share our commitment to that vision.

In the end, clarity in our purpose and path ensures those who walk with us truly belong on this journey. And for those who part ways, we offer our sincere gratitude and respect, knowing that each path, no matter how divergent, contributes to the rich tapestry of our collective experiences.

Navigating Scalability Challenges

Let's assume for a moment that your strategy, powered by the PATH framework, is a resounding success. You and your team are making all the right choices and your organization is thriving and growing.

But with growth comes a new set of challenges, as growth isn't solely about scaling up in size. The increase in complexity can quietly start to cloud the clear, straightforward PATH that once set the foundation for your organization's success.

Maintaining Strategic Integrity in Expansion: The Power of No

In the early days, decisions are made swiftly, processes are lean, and the strategic path is clear. However, as your organization expands, a streamlined operation can gradually become a complex labyrinth. Procedures that were straightforward turn into multilayered operations, bureaucracy increases, and the workforce diversifies, with more voices, opinions, and stakeholder interests.

In this larger organizational context, how do you preserve the straightforwardness of how you make choices?

Growing organizations almost inevitably develop more complex structures. There's not much you can do to avoid this. But the way you build it, the choices you make—not *while* you scale but about *how* you scale—are crucial to maintaining strategic simplicity. The key lies in distilling a thousand choices down to one: staying on your PATH even as you grow.

And that often means saying no. Steve Jobs, the visionary behind Apple, famously emphasized the importance of saying no. He believed that focusing isn't about saying no to the things you wouldn't want to do anyway, but about saying no to the things you would wholeheartedly love to do or think you have to do out of necessity.

For Apple, this meant making tough choices, often forgoing attractive opportunities that didn't align with their core vision. In your organization, this principle translates into a selective focus on initiatives and projects that truly align with your PATH and propel your core mission forward.

Sometimes, this approach requires sacrificing good ideas in favor of great ones that are more aligned with your strategic PATH. Resources are finite, after all, and spreading them too thinly in multiple directions can dilute your strategic impact. Scaling in alignment could mean saying no to a new branch, a new hire, or even a new idea unless you can clearly articulate how that choice allows you to get further on your PATH.

A well-crafted PATH replaces constant decision-making struggles with a clear, overarching direction and a shared understanding of what right choices look like. It serves as a North Star, not only in the things your organization does, but also in *how* it does them. The framework becomes the lens through which every potential action is evaluated, including the ones that relate to the very structure of your business.

As your organization grows, the discipline to say no to diversions keeps you on track, with the simplicity and focus that sparked your initial success. Even in the face of expansion, your organization stays true to its foundational principles and continues to move forward with purpose and clarity. In fact, for Apple, this was essential to becoming one of the world's biggest businesses. It can be for you, too.

Dealing with Organizational Diversity: Trust Your Team

And yet, despite all efforts to keep it simple, the more your organization scales, the less a one-size-fits-all approach is feasible. It's unlikely that a simple statement will answer every question in every part of your organization. The PATH, while serving as a unified guide, needs to be adapted to resonate across the wide spectrum of your organization.

For example, FedEx's commitment to "absolutely, positively overnight" delivery meant different things for different parts of the organization. For logistics, it was about efficiency in delivery routes; for customer service, it was about informing and reassuring clients about their deliveries; and for the frontline workers, it was about empowering them to make swift decisions in the best interest of their customers.

This requires rather specific choices. Someone needs to make them.

The key to scaling well is understanding that that person *doesn't have to be you*. You don't have to make all the choices yourself, nor do you have to define a perfect rule set that covers every special case. Actually, it's almost the opposite. The fewer of these choices you make yourself, the better.

Think of it this way: Leadership defines the overall PATH and crafts company-wide traffic rules for how to travel it. You supply your team with different vehicles, each designed for its specific terrain: for example nimble bikes for quick, tactical decisions or steady trucks for longer-term strategies. But *you don't drive these vehicles*. Your team does.

One of the worst things that can happen to a business is when the leader becomes the bottleneck of decision-making. It slows everything down and can be utterly frustrating for the teams. Scaling successfully involves recognizing that these choices are best made by those closest to the action, but within the boundaries of the overall PATH.

Just like an architect trusts builders to translate blueprints into tangible structures, you trust your teams to interpret and apply the PATH framework in ways that align with their functions.

Here's the good news: When the PATH is plain and simple, actionable, transformative, and heartfelt, you can trust your team with making those choices within their domains. You allow your organization to operate within a shared vision while leveraging the unique strengths and insights of each team.

This balance of guidance and autonomy is key to maintaining strategic coherence amidst diversity. It ensures that while your organization grows in size, it also grows in strategic depth, effectiveness, and unity.

Maintaining Flexibility

One word of caution, though: Even the most robust and well-defined strategies may require course adjustments—not as admissions of failure, but as essential acts of strategic agility. These adjustments recognize that the business landscape is ever-changing and demand that your strategy flexes and evolves in response.

You don't have to (or want to) chase every trend, but some changes must not be ignored—like shifts in economies, technological advancements, or shifting societal needs. Rigidly sticking to an unaltered strategy can be more limiting than empowering.

But how can you balance consistency and flexibility, making sure your strategic PATH remains as dynamic and alive as the market in which you operate?

Switching Lanes

Consider the remarkable evolution of Netflix. Netflix's decisions to first embrace streaming and then invest heavily in original content were not just reactions to market changes; they were proactive steps to stay ahead.

Their initial success in DVD rentals was significant, but the company recognized the limitations of this model earlier than many others. Instead of clinging to the familiar, they foresaw the potential for streaming and adjusted their strategy in anticipation of market trends. They did the same thing again by investing in original content.

As disruptive as these transitions may look from the outside, that might not be how it looked from the inside. Netflix's business was never about "being the market leaders in DVD rental." It was about "entertaining the world." Both their major adjustments stayed perfectly aligned with this PATH.

This broader vision allowed them to transcend traditional boundaries where others would have stuck with their existing business model. They could embrace streaming because it was aligned with their PATH. Ultimately, DVD rentals were just one possible *lane* on their entertainment PATH.

The decision to pivot reflected an understanding of where the entertainment industry was headed. In a way, they were simply doing their job. Their actions, though risky, demonstrated a commitment to their PATH and ensured their strategy remained relevant and competitive.

Re-considering Your PATH

Contrast this with Kodak. Despite inventing the first digital camera, Kodak hesitated to embrace digital technology fully, fearing it would cannibalize their film business. Their PATH was about making film, not capturing moments, and so they weren't ready or willing to move towards digital.

This reluctance led to their steep decline, overshadowed by competitors who readily embraced digital innovation. Kodak's story is a cautionary tale of how sticking rigidly to a traditional path, even when it leads to a dead end, can have significant consequences.

But that's the reality. Sometimes, the landscape of business presents scenarios that are radically different from our expectations. Certain paths that once seemed promising may be too narrow for the expanding scale of your organization, if not lead to dead ends. You'd be a fool not to re-consider your PATH.

Flexibility isn't a sign of weakness. It's an attribute of strategic foresight and strength.

As your business grows, continuously assess the viability of your current strategies. Are they scalable? Do they align with emerging market trends? Sometimes, what worked for a smaller-scale operation doesn't hold up in a larger context.

Be vigilant about recognizing signs that a particular strategy or direction is no longer viable. These could be diminishing returns, market saturation, or disruptive technological innovations that render your current path obsolete.

The decision to change course requires courage and a clear-eyed assessment of the situation. But it's necessary because sticking to a path just for the sake of consistency will be detrimental if that path no longer leads to growth or relevance.

Had Kodak redefined its PATH to focus on capturing moments rather than making film, they might have embraced the shift to digital decisively. It would merely have been a different lane on the same, but broader, PATH.

In your journey, be prepared to reassess and realign your PATH with an evolving market so your PATH remains relevant and effective. What looks like a change of direction might turn out to be just another lane on a bigger PATH.

Unless, of course, the full change of direction is the right thing to do ...

Changing Direction

While consistency is valuable, it shouldn't restrict your freedom to explore new horizons, especially given that not every pivot is a reaction to external pressures. Some are proactive and deliberate strategic choices. Being overly rigid on the PATH you set years ago can mean missing out on extraordinary opportunities that arise along the way.

Amazon made a decisive shift into cloud computing when they saw that the infrastructure they had built for themselves presented an incredible business opportunity. They weren't bound by their original PATH but were flexible enough to explore and capitalize on these new opportunities, fundamentally changing their trajectory.

If you're solely fixated on defending the PATH you've chosen, you risk overlooking the right time to pivot. Focus doesn't mean having total blinders on to what's on the left or right; it simply helps you stay the course among stressful moments or distractions such as shiny trends. But there may come a time when turning to the left or right is the right choice.

That choice to keep your focus or make a real pivot is made easier by following the PATH principles:

>**Is it plain and simple?** Can you clearly articulate what the choice is?

>**Is it actionable?** Do you have a clear understanding of what the right choices are in your new direction?

>**Is it transformative?** Does the opportunity have the potential for you to make a bigger impact than you do now, and will it motivate you and your team to explore that terrain?

>**Is it heartfelt?** Does it align with your core values, and will your team not only understand but wholeheartedly embrace your new direction?

This can (but doesn't have to) mean turning your whole business around. For example, when Nokia entered the mobile phone market, it left most of its other business, such as the manufacturing of rubber boots, behind to become the world's dominant mobile phone manufacturer.

But it can also mean diversifying your business, as it did for Amazon when it entered the cloud computing industry.

Change *does* happen. Ultimately, it's less important to be right about the initial PATH than it is to get it right as you move. The PATH principles provide you with a framework to make informed choices at each crossroads.

The world of business is dynamic; new opportunities and challenges will emerge. Staying open to change and being willing to consider these new avenues can lead to unprecedented growth and success. Let your PATH be a living, evolving entity, one that guides you but also grows with you.

Conclusion

In this chapter, we have traversed the complex dynamics of organizational life, acknowledging that the road to strategic clarity and impact is often paved with tough decisions, resistance, and even moments of doubt. However, it is within these very challenges that the true strength and adaptability of the PATH framework—and your leadership—are tested and proven.

Remember, navigating your PATH is not about rigid adherence to a predetermined route; it's about maintaining your strategic integrity while being open to course corrections and new learnings. It's about balancing the steadfast pursuit of your vision with the agility to respond to new insights and shifting circumstances.

As you move forward, embrace the challenges as opportunities for growth and refinement. Treat each obstacle as a stepping stone that deepens your understanding and commitment to your strategic objectives. Encourage openness and candid feedback within your team and foster an environment where every voice can contribute to the collective journey.

Above all, let your PATH be a source of inspiration and guidance for your team. Your unwavering commitment to the PATH principles—being Plain and Simple, Actionable, Transformative, and Heartfelt—will serve as a beacon, guiding your team through complexity and change. It will help create a culture where challenges are met with creativity, resilience, and a shared sense of purpose.

8

Lighting the PATH

The discovery of your PATH might be a pivotal moment for you and your leadership team, but the true test is how eager your team will be to join you. After all, the journey to strategic impact is not a solitary trek but a shared expedition. To make it work, it's not enough for *you* to see and believe in the PATH—your *team* must see the PATH and believe in it just as passionately as you do.

Can you transcend the role of the planner and strategic thinker to become the beacon that lights the PATH for the whole team? Using words that compel your team to walk it with you?

This means creating a bond, a shared belief in the PATH to your common destination, where every step taken is not out of obligation, but out of a genuine desire to be part of something bigger than oneself.

It's the opposite of towing a line that forces the team to move together. Therefore, your most powerful tool is not authority, but inspiration—kindling a spark within each team member that ignites a collective drive towards realizing your organization's vision.

Filling the PATH with Meaning

Imagine standing in front of your team, unveiling the new strategic PATH. The room is filled with anticipation, but also a hint of skepticism. You're bursting with pride, having condensed your strategy into crisp, clear statements that are plain and simple, actionable, transformative, and deeply heartfelt. They're the perfect summary of your detailed underlying playbook.

But they're also just words. A skeleton that, without further explanation, can be fleshed out in very different ways by different members of your organization. It's clearly insufficient to simply unveil and list them. They need to be filled with consistent meaning.

In other words, your team needs to see the PATH just as clearly and vividly as you do. Picture an artist bringing a canvas to life. Each brushstroke adds depth, emotion, and clarity to what was once a mere sketch. Your strategic PATH is that sketch and, like the sketch on the canvas, now demands the same artistry.

In business, this is where the art of storytelling becomes your most powerful tool. Howard Schultz, the former CEO of Starbucks, used it to flesh out their strategy of becoming the "third place between home and work." His storytelling revolved around the experience and culture of Starbucks, and he would often share stories about individual stores, baristas, or customer experiences, emphasizing the community and connection fostered by the Starbucks brand.

Here are some examples of how he did this:

1. *The Italian espresso bar **inspiration***: Schultz often recounted his visit to Italy and how the Italian espresso bars influenced him. He spoke about the culture of these bars, where people gather, talk, and enjoy coffee in a relaxed, inviting atmosphere. This experience was a key inspiration for what he envisioned Starbucks could become—a place beyond just coffee, offering a sense of community and belonging.

2. *Personal stories of **connection***: Schultz shared stories of interactions between Starbucks baristas and customers, highlighting how these connections went beyond transactions. He would talk about baristas remembering a regular customer's drink order or small details about their lives, fostering a sense of personal connection.

3. *Creating a culture of **belonging***: Schultz often narrated stories about what Starbucks stood for—a place where everyone, regardless of background, was welcome. He reinforced this with stories of Starbucks' involvement in community events, support for local causes, or initiatives like hiring veterans and refugees, emphasizing its role as a community hub.

4. *Stories that inspire **innovation and evolution***: Schultz used stories of Starbucks' evolution, like the introduction of new products or the Starbucks mobile app, to demonstrate how the company was innovating

while staying true to its core value of creating a welcoming "third place" for customers.

5. *Stories that foster employee **empowerment***: Schultz shared anecdotes about empowering employees (referred to as partners) and how their contributions shaped the company. Stories of baristas contributing ideas that became successful or how they went above and beyond to make customers' days better were common, illustrating the ethos of the "third place" being as much about the people who work there as those who visit.

These stories filled the "third place" with a concrete meaning. Not only did they exemplify what a "third place" looks like, they were also easy to share, carrying the meaning with them as they traveled through the organization.

Schultz didn't just sell a naked idea; he wove a narrative people could see themselves in. Through these stories he created a place they could belong, a place that was filled with a *culture*, not just a vision and some random rules. He transformed the strategic PATH of Starbucks from a series of corporate goals into a living, breathing ethos that resonated deeply with employees and customers alike.

In your organization, seek to do the same. Use storytelling to breathe life into your PATH, making it not only a strategy but a shared journey that everyone is eager to join. Show your team not just the map, but why the journey matters and how they each play a crucial role in it.

Can They See it?

Throughout this book, we've asked, "Can you see it?" Here, we're essentially asking that again, but with a twist. This time we're asking, "Can *the team* see it?"

The stories that bring your PATH to life are not the stories of your heroic efforts in figuring out the PATH. They are the stories of your team's heroic efforts in walking that path. Step off the hero's pedestal and leave it to your team. The real power of a good story is in the fact that we can identify with it. That's why Schultz's stories about individual stores, baristas, or customer experiences worked so well. It's the hero we look at, but—as a Starbucks employee—it's ourselves who we see in that role. *We* could have been the barista who brought a smile to the customer's face.

That's what you need to aim for: giving your team that feeling of empowerment. "This could be me! I could make these choices and have a profound influence on the course of our organization."

So the goal is to connect emotionally and make it tangible for those who have to make the choices in their everyday lives. Stories achieve this by showing us how it's been done previously, how people similar to us have made similar choices to those we need to make on our journey.

For example:

> **The inspiring customer interaction**: Share real stories from the team or use inspiring stories from everyday life to fill your PATH with meaning.
>
> **The shared spirit**: The story of an employee who stayed late, experimenting, until they cracked a problem that

revolutionized a product. Let us feel the grit—the eureka moment—that comes with making a leap on the PATH.

The feeling of belonging: Make us feel the pain of having to make a tough choice and how that choice defines who we are.

The shared aspirations: What's your version of the Italian espresso bar?

The best stories are those where the Core Credo shines through. When the Core Credo gets passed along and everyone thinks of the same stories, that's what shapes your organization's culture. It's as simple as that.

And, yes, simplicity is key here.

A final word: While stories often are, by far, the most powerful tool to fill your PATH with life, other tools may help, too, such as visualizations, checklists, or working procedures. The crucial point here is to use them on an as-needed basis. Don't overwhelm every member on your team with a checklist, when it's only relevant for a specific domain. Be specific, keep it simple, and fill it with concrete meaning for those who have to make the choice.

The key question to keep in mind is: Can *they* see it?

Ingraining Your PATH into Your Culture

But, of course, it's not enough to light the path just once. You need to keep the lights on every single step of the way.

Think of your PATH as a rhythm, a beat that resonates through the entire organization. The more frequently it's heard, the more it becomes ingrained in the collective consciousness.

Your consistent reiteration of the Core Credo is more than a reminder; it's a tool for embedding these principles deeply into the daily fabric of your organization. Each repetition serves as an echo, reinforcing your PATH, reminding every team member of the journey you're all on together.

Mapping Current Events to Your PATH

An effective approach for embedding your PATH in your organization's culture is to continuously map current events, successes, and even challenges back to it. Celebrate successes by highlighting how they exemplify the principles of your PATH. When challenges arise, use them as opportunities to demonstrate your PATH's relevance and resilience.

For instance, if you're in a team meeting, discussing a recent success, tie it back to how it exemplifies being actionable or transformative according to your PATH. If you're addressing a setback, discuss it in the context of heartfelt decision-making or the need to return to plain and simple solutions.

Remember, too, that your PATH isn't static. It evolves with your organization. This evolution should be communicated just as clearly, showing your team that while the core values remain, the application can adapt to changing circumstances.

Keeping the Lights on

The point is to keep the lights on, night and day. Your PATH informs the choices your team needs to make, but only if it's top of mind when they need to make them. You need to communicate it not only clearly, but frequently.

The Core Credo deserves that name only when it becomes the actual credo that permanently echoes through the organization. This could be through newsletters, team meetings, or even informal conversations. But the most powerful amplifiers are the people themselves. Inspiring them to pass the Core Credo along creates a ripple effect that reaches even the tiniest corner of your organization.

The power of the Core Credo is that it's so short and to the point that it can be easily integrated into your regular communication. When your team sees your PATH being referred to consistently, they start viewing it not just as a concept or as pretty words, but as a living, breathing aspect of their work environment, lit by the stories you share that fill it with meaning.

As a leader, your unwavering commitment to your PATH sets the tone. Your team will take cues from your dedication. If they see you passionately and consistently advocating for your PATH, they will mirror this commitment. Your role is to be the beacon, lighting your PATH, so it remains visible and clear at all times.

The PATH that Shapes Your Culture

But it's not just about repetition. If your PATH is really heartfelt, then it will have the power to shape your culture.

It's the very essence of how you make choices. It's the driving force behind your progress. It's what motivates and empowers your team.

This requires:

> **Embedding it in processes**: Integrate your PATH into your decision-making processes, performance evaluations, and even recruitment strategies.
>
> **Training and development**: Offer regular training sessions that reinforce your PATH principles and how they can be applied in various roles.

Celebration and recognition: Acknowledge and celebrate when individuals or teams exemplify the PATH in their actions and decisions.

Ingraining the PATH into your organization's culture means more than just alignment; it means fostering a community where the PATH principles are the heartbeat of every decision and action.

Not Compliance, but Connection

In a sunlit, spacious office, a team gathers around a large, circular table. The walls are adorned with photos and quotes, each a testament to a shared experience. As the meeting begins, there's a buzz of energy, not the usual mundane shuffle of papers and hushed tones.

A project manager stands up, her eyes alight with excitement. She's not just outlining the next project; she's sharing a new idea that's close to her heart. Her passion is infectious. Her words paint a picture of what could be. This project isn't just another task on a checklist; it's a chance to make a real difference, to innovate, to push boundaries. But is it the right thing to do?

A discussion follows. Plenty of good reasons stand on each side of the argument. But this is about more than profit margins or market share; it's about impact, passion, and the legacy they yearn to leave in the world. The conversation shifts from what is safe to what is right, from fear to possibility. The choice is hard. The stakes feel high. Yet, as they debate, a transformation occurs. The fear of the unknown becomes a collective resolve to strive for something greater, to make a leap on the PATH everyone has committed themselves to.

The decision is made. It's bold, daunting. But as they stand together, there's a sense of exhilaration, of stepping into a future they choose to shape. The room is charged with energy and a sense of unity and purpose. It's clear that everyone here is not just working on a project. They're part of a journey that goes beyond the confines of the office walls. They are connected, not just by their work but by a shared ethos, a commitment to excellence, and a belief in the power of what they can achieve together.

Imagine that this is your workplace. That it doesn't function on compliance but thrives on connection. That your team doesn't follow your PATH out of duty but embraces it with fervor and passion. That your PATH is more than a strategy—it's a shared journey, enriched by individual stories and collective successes that transcend into a living culture.

If done right, if you truly light the PATH, alignment doesn't have to be enforced. It will be wholeheartedly embraced by your team as a part of your organizational identity.

Lighting the PATH is not about persuading people to walk the PATH—it's about resonating with them so strongly that they choose to travel it with enthusiasm and dedication.

This is when the PATH enables positive impact.

It changes everything.

Can you see it?

9

True Progress

Visions define what we aspire for. But the true measure of our vision is not in how high we aim. What counts is how far we progress on our journey towards those heights. It's the *strategy, communicated effectively and acted upon collectively*, that transforms aspirations into realities.

The PATH we've laid out is as literal as it is metaphorical. It's the route along which every leader and team member walks, making choices that propel your organization in a clear strategic direction.

When you, dear reader, light that PATH using the principles introduced in this book, your strategy becomes truly impactful. Simply ask four essential questions: Is it plain and simple? Actionable? Transformative? And heartfelt?

With compelling answers to these questions, you'll see a surge in clarity and unity.

Decision-making will become more intuitive and aligned, enabling your company to execute strategies faster and spend resources more wisely.

You'll encourage bold moves that enhance your brand's prestige, leap you ahead of the competition, and potentially redefine industry rules.

Your team's deep connection to their work will boost productivity and creativity, strengthen customer satisfaction and loyalty, and secure long-term sustainability.

What a contrast to the picture we began this book with, which is still the norm in so many organizations! Now, your strategy can fuel true progress.

Your PATH is the road upon which legacies are built and the trail that, when lit with clarity and purpose, leads you to the realization of your most ambitious dreams.

Keep lighting the PATH!

Appendix

Appendix A

The PATH to Strategic Impact in a Nutshell

You've got a bold vision and a smart strategy! But how do you get your team to act on it? How do you align the thousands of tiny choices each member in the organization has to make every day to realize the strategy? In other words: How do you light the PATH for your team?

PATH is an acronym that combines four principles to help you turn strategy communication into a powerful decision-making tool: Plain and Simple, Actionable, Transformative and Heartfelt.

The four PATH principles help you get your strategy communication right, identify holes in your communication, and even spot weaknesses in your strategy (so that you can fix them). You will empower every team member, from the ground up, to make the right choices with clarity and conviction so they can understand, participate in, and drive forward the strategic vision.

1. Plain and Simple

Answer the simple question "What is our strategy all about?" in plain English!

In a nutshell: *Strip away the jargon, speak a language everyone understands, and capture it in a Core Credo. When you get this right, your strategy will get passed along and morph into your company's culture, guiding behaviors even when not explicitly stated.*

Helpful questions:

- What is our core strategic message in one sentence?

- Does our strategy avoid industry jargon in favor of plain English, with clear and universally understood terms?

- Can our team members (at all levels) articulate the strategy in their own words without losing its essence?

- Is our Core Credo reflected in daily conversations and decisions across the organization?

- Are new employees able to grasp our strategic direction quickly?

Your thoughts: _____

_____

_____

_____

_____

2. Actionable

Make the right choice stand out as if it were the only one!

In a nutshell: *Ensure the strategy can guide day-to-day decisions and actions and foster an intuitive understanding of the right choices. The true value of an actionable strategy lies in its ability to light the path so distinctly that choices don't just become easier, they become obvious.*

Helpful questions:

- Do we focus on actions as opposed to outcomes?
- Are our team members able to independently translate the strategy into actions without having to consult leadership?
- Can everyone on the team describe in plain English what a choice that aligns with our strategy looks like?
- Does our strategy provide a clear direction when faced with uncertain or complex situations?
- Do we collect and share examples of where our strategy has illuminated clear and obvious choices?

Your thoughts: _____

_____

_____

_____

_____

_____

3. Transformative

Encourage your team to confidently make bold choices!

In a nutshell: *Declare that the status quo is no longer enough. A transformative strategy is the force that makes your team want to walk the PATH. It's the robust voice over the murmurs of hesitation, the firm hand that guides your team not only towards doing different things, but doing things differently.*

Helpful questions:

- What significant change or impact do we aim to achieve with our strategy?
- Do we encourage bold moves and decisive action?
- Do our team members see how their actions will make a difference?
- Is that difference aligned with their personal motivations?
- What behaviors or cultural shifts are we expecting or encouraging?
- What success stories can we share that exemplify transformative results?

Your thoughts: _____

_____

_____

_____

4. Heartfelt

Find words that your team truly believes in about the things they deeply care about!

In a nutshell: *Connect emotionally. A strategy that endures is one that is felt deeply. It answers the soul-searching question of "Why us?" It's the genuine passion for your collective mission that lights up the PATH, not just for the mind to follow, but for the heart to lead.*

Helpful questions:

- Do our team members feel a personal and emotional connection to the actions our strategy encourages?
- Does our strategy contribute to a greater purpose and align with the underlying "Why" of our organization?
- Are the words we use heartfelt and passionate or dry and corporate?
- Do we trust our team with making choices?
- How do we celebrate achievements in a way that resonates with our team's values?

Your thoughts: _____

_____

_____

_____

_____

_____

Implementation and Review

Don't persuade: resonate!

In a nutshell: *Light the PATH with clarity! Regularly revisit these principles to ensure the strategy remains dynamic, relevant, and deeply integrated into the fabric of the organization.*

Helpful questions:

- How do we communicate and reinforce the PATH principles in our everyday operations?

- Do we use stories and provide additional resources to make the abstract concrete and to fill our PATH with meaning?

- What practices do we have to ensure the PATH principles are consistently applied across all levels of our organization?

- How frequently do we review our strategy for alignment with the PATH principles?

- What forums or platforms do we use for open discussion and feedback on our strategy?

- How do we adapt our strategy in response to new insights or market changes?

Find more resources on the book's website: https://michaelgerharz.com/the-path/resources

Appendix B

Glossary
From Vision to Strategy

Terms like vision, mission, and strategy are a frequent source of confusion. They're omnipresent, but often used without a clear definition. Here's what they mean in this book:

Vision

That's your big dream of a better future. It's called "vision" because you visualize what a better world will look like so that you can see it very clearly. The will to make that vision a reality is the driving force for everything you do. In a way, it's the destination of your organization's journey.

Mission

You embark on a mission to make the vision a reality. Each mission has a specific goal. That goal can be as ambitious as realizing your complete vision, but it can also be a part of it. You can think of a mission as a journey towards realizing (parts of) your vision.

Strategy

To fulfill your mission, you choose a strategy. A strategy is a commitment to how you want to make choices while you're on the journey of your mission. It informs you how to make those choices by providing guidelines and boundaries.

PATH

PATH is a tool to help you communicate your strategy. In an ideal world, your strategy creates a path to your mission's goal and, ultimately, to realizing your vision. By lighting that path, you empower your team to make the right choices. As introduced in this book, PATH is a set of four principles that help you evaluate how good your strategy communication is at lighting the path. The four principles are Plain and Simple, Actionable, Transformative, and Heartfelt.

Tactics

Tactics are specific choices you make within the limits of your strategy. Those choices can be made by you or by someone from your team.

Purpose

Your purpose is the why of your vision. It tells you why that vision will be a worthwhile reality.

Appendix C

Further Reading

Here's a short list of books—in alphabetic order—that I've found useful throughout my career in helping me and my clients make sense of strategy, leadership, communication, and human behavior.

Belonging: Unlock Your Potential with the Ancient Code of Togetherness
Owen Eastwood
Insights from a sports performance coach on what happens when team members find a sense of belonging to something greater than themselves.

Essentialism: The Disciplined Pursuit of Less
Greg McKeown
What focus really means and why it matters.

Good To Great: Why Some Companies Make the Leap... and Others Don't
Jim Collins
Lessons from 30 companies that made the leap from good to great.

Made to Stick: Why Some Ideas Survive and Others Die
Chip Heath & Dan Heath
Lessons from some of history's most successful communication campaigns and what they mean for communicating ideas that stick.

Meaningful: The Story of Ideas That Fly
Bernadette Jiwa
An inspirational book about doing work that matters.

Moments of Impact: How to Design Strategic Conversations That Accelerate Change
Chris Ertel & Lisa Kay Solomon
An insightful book on how to run better meetings.

Multipliers: How the Best Leaders Make Everyone Smarter
Liz Wiseman
Observations on what happens when leaders put the spotlight on the team and help them do better than they imagined.

No Bullsh*t Strategy: A Founder's Guide to Gaining Competitive Advantage with a Strategy That Actually Works
Alex M H Smith
A refreshing take on strategy, stripping away the terminological overhead of many other books and using plain and simple English to make sense of strategy.

Playing to Win: How Strategy Really Works
A.G. Lafley, Roger L. Martin
Insights from one of the world's biggest and most successful companies on how they approach strategy.

The Coaching Habit: Say Less, Ask More & Change the Way You Lead Forever
Michael Bungay Stanier
An inspirational book that challenges the idea that leaders should have the answers and instead promotes asking better questions.

Leaders Light the Path Manifesto
Dr. Michael Gerharz
A short piece I wrote on a more modern approach to leadership. Access it for free at https://LeadersLightThePath.com.

The Power of Habit: Why We Do What We Do, and How to Change
Charles Duhigg
An insightful look into how habits work, why it's so hard to change them, and how we might do so.

Thinking, Fast and Slow
Daniel Kahneman
Probably the best book on decision-making you'll find.

Thinking in Bets: Making Smarter Decisions When You Don't Have All the Facts
Annie Duke
Lessons from a world-class poker player about making (and evaluating) choices in uncertainty.

Start with Why: How Great Leaders Inspire Everyone to Take Action
Simon Sinek
The classic book that introduced the golden circle of how-what-why.

Where Good Ideas Come From: The Natural History of Innovation
Steven Johnson
A book on how to create the conditions for good ideas to be discovered.

Acknowledgments

This book wouldn't exist without these brilliant people:

My wife, Stephanie, is my best friend and most trusted advisor. Thanks for being on that journey together. Your support means the world to me.

Thanks to my three wonderful kids, who, despite being teenagers, had so many insightful things to say that it makes me unbelievably proud to be their dad.

And many thanks to my mum, Regina, to Hans, and to my brother, Stephan, for joining me on my path to where I am today.

Thanks to these wonderful friends and colleagues: Lukas Pustina for your thoughtful comments. Shane Cradock for your thought-provoking questions. Tim Huelin and Jobien Hekking for your ever-present support and encouragement. Marie-Claire Junge, Kathy Letendre, and Françoise Hontoy for your critical eyes. Ariana Friedlander, Antonia Mahon, Jackie Lopey, Pamela Benham, and Casey von Neumann for pushing me further. Ed Prow for your kindness and ambition.

Thanks to my editor, Hannah de Keijzer, who relentlessly pushed me to find better words; my proofreader, Yasmin Yarwood, who chased the tiniest comma; my designer, Rachel Valliere, who turned the text into a piece of beauty; and my publishing manager, Katya Fishman, who helped the book see the light of day.

Thanks to my wonderful clients, who continue to make an impact on their customers' lives and allow me to witness the power of great communication.

Finally, this book is standing on the shoulders of the great teachers I've met in my life.

I'm grateful for having crossed the path of these phenomenal people.

Thanks to all of you for lighting the path!

About the Author

Dr. Michael Gerharz helps leaders across the globe find the right words and make a bigger impact.

Michael earned his Ph.D. in Communication Systems during the mobile phone revolution, observing firsthand how brilliant ideas die when people fail or don't care to communicate them properly. Seeing these missed opportunities, he decided to do something about it, launched his blog, and carved a career path dedicated to mastering and teaching the art of communication.

Today, Michael helps leaders communicate with irresistible clarity so their ideas can make the impact they deserve. He guides clients to find words they truly believe in about the things they deeply care about, and his insights and strategies have transformed communication practices in numerous organizations, making him a sought-after expert in the field.

His first book, *The AHA Effect*, is a heartfelt call for audience-focused communication. Too many communicators are in it for the applause rather than the impact. But what use is a great show or fancy wording when it doesn't change your audience's mind? The aha effect beats the wow effect every single time, and this book shows you how to achieve and lead your own audiences to insight.

He is also the author of the *Leaders Light the Path Manifesto* and writes the blog *The Art of Communicating,* where leaders from around the world access daily thoughts that help them find the right words. His podcast, *Irresistible Communication,* is listened to in 90+ countries.

A passionate guitarist, Michael works at the intersection of highly structured thinking and the pure joy of creative expression.

You can find out more about his services at https://michael gerharz.com.

Get Your Strategy Communication Right!

Finding the right words to communicate your strategy is no small task. While the PATH principles themselves are simple, that doesn't mean implementing them will be.

I've assembled a number of resources to help you:

RESOURCES ON THE BOOK'S WEBSITE

The book's website hosts an extensive list of resources that will help you choose and implement the PATH principles in your own business. This includes checklists, case studies, and a self-assessment to help you see where your strategy communication is doing well and where it can lead to stronger outcomes and a more motivated team.

YOU'LL FIND EVERYTHING AT
https://michaelgerharz.com/the-path/resources.

CLARIFYING QUESTIONS

Communication is a two-way street, and I would love this book to embody that. If you have a clarifying question about any of the concepts and ideas in this book, don't hesitate to shoot an email to the-path@michaelgerharz.com, call me on +49 (2241) 899-7777, or connect on LinkedIn. I trust you to be responsible with this offer.

Of course, I would very much love to hear back from you if you've found the book useful or if it has led to a breakthrough.

COMMUNICATION ADVISORY

If you want my support in making the PATH principles work for you, contact me via email at **the-path@michaelgerharz.com** or call me on **+49 (2241) 899-7777**.

Printed in Great Britain
by Amazon